The Two Faces of Education

An Insider's View of School Reform

Michael I. Allen

Rowman & Littlefield Education
Lanham, Maryland • Toronto • Oxford
2006

Published in the United States of America
by Rowman & Littlefield Education
A Division of Rowman & Littlefield Publishers, Inc.
A wholly owned subsidary of The Rowman & Littlefield Publishing Group, Inc.
4501 Forbes Boulevard, Suite 200, Lanham, Maryland 20706
www.rowmaneducation.com

PO Box 317
Oxford
OX2 9RU, UK

British Library Cataloguing in Publication Information Available

Library of Congress Cataloging-in-Publication Data

Allen, Michael I., 1965–
    The two faces of education : an insider's view of school reform / Michael I.
Allen.
        p. cm.
    Includes bibliographical references.
    ISBN-13: 978-1-57886-397-6 (hardcover : alk. paper)
    ISBN-10: 1-57886-397-X (hardcover : alk. paper)
    ISBN-13: 978-1-57886-406-5 (pbk. : alk. paper)
    ISBN-10: 1-57886-406-2 (pbk. : alk. paper)
    1. Teaching—United States. 2. Teacher-student relationships—United States.
3. Educational change—United States. I. Title.

LB1775.2.A443 2006
371.1—dc22   2005031474

CONTENTS

ACKNOWLEDGMENTS

I would like to thank the following people for offering support and encouragement and enabling me to complete this book:

My sister Valerie Allen, Monica Allen, Judith Baker, Sandra Barefoot, Pat Bonarrigo, Patricia Brown, Charles Burgess for his mentoring, Michelle Madera Cepada, Carol Denker, William Flight, Debra Fox, Paul Hajjar Esq., Katie Johnson, Ellie Kelley, Robert Klieman, Lou Larry, Brandy Manza, Toni Marsh, Joe Mascarotolo, Chuck McAfee, Patricia Melanson, Jeff Riley, Helaine Sanches, Jose Solis, Sarah Teasdale, Parry Teasdale, and Junia Yearwood.

Illustrations by Abu Troy Sammah.

A special thank-you to Paul Nichols for his editing.

To my wife, Donna Allen, thank you for everything. Your words of encouragement motivated and inspired me more than you will ever know.

INTRODUCTION

As a teacher and an administrator, I have experienced my fair share of bizarre situations. I must continually remind myself to find the humor in each moment. If I did not reflect on the past and chuckle to myself, I would either become a candidate for Bellevue Hospital or spend a lot of time crying. These strange events have twisted my view of education and changed my reasons for staying in this field. I have seen my children arrive at school with mental scars, broken hearts, and empty stomachs. I feel helpless, knowing that I am unable to change what has slowly become the status quo. Student after student has approached me for help, since I am one of the few reliable people to ever cross their path. Society expects me as an educator to "leave no child behind" and to work tirelessly to improve every child's educational opportunity. Yet I am a fallible human, capable of making mistakes. The undue pressure I've placed on myself to achieve and to be available to help my students is stressful and very hard not to take home.

I went to college at the University of Vermont where I studied under eminent scholars of education. Even though I was preparing for a career in occupation extension technology, my professors made sure I understood how to promote literacy across the curriculum and how to recognize the political landscape of national trends. But like most schools, the university failed to teach me how to handle the social or emotional inequities many students face today.

I remember doing some substitute teaching in college. I had the pleasure of working with an excellent industrial arts teacher. He was preparing me to take over his class for a week while he engaged in professional development. I had substituted for him several times before, and we had built a mutual respect. I was taking attendance and noticed that one child was constantly missing school. I asked Mr. Paul, "Where is Trina?"

Mr. Paul responded by saying, "Let's just say that her mother has been renting her out."

Although my students come to school with severe social and emotional problems, they are held to high standards and are expected to develop and to extend their capabilities as productive citizens. I look at the luggage my students drag with them to school each day and wonder why some of them even bother. This book is about the luggage the students carry; luggage that was either placed on them or created by them. We commonly refer to people's problems as baggage. But my students have luggage—of the old Samsonite variety. An elephant can stand on it and it won't break. The only way to get into it is with a key, which unfortunately is kept tucked away and must somehow be located first.

I hope my readers learn to find the humor in this enigma and appreciate what educators do beyond teaching children the basics. As dedicated educators, we look to instill the hope of finding the key to success, while imparting knowledge or the necessary push that helps all students surpass their own expectations.

All of the stories in this book are true. Even original 911 calls are transcribed as closely to the original recording as possible. All of the names have been changed to protect the innocent—and not so innocent.

WHEN A FIFTH GRADER ATTACKS

After completing college, I faced the daunting task of finding a job. Like everyone else in the field of education, I wanted to find a teaching position. My brother knew of a temporary job as a teacher's assistant in an elementary school classroom working with emotionally disturbed and learning disabled students. The placement was not the kind of job I wanted, but it paid a few bills and gave me some health benefits.

One month into the job, I was informed that I was required to receive training in crisis prevention intervention (CPI). The training was mandated due to the children's behavior. The sessions lasted seven hours, except for the last day, which was a testing day and lasted only an hour. I was able to go back to work by late morning. At the end of the day my supervising teacher, Janis Carpenter, and I escorted the third through fifth grade classes to their bus. As we stood by the exit, we heard screams coming from a young male. Seconds later, his screams sharpened into obscenities.

I asked Ms. Carpenter, "Do you want me to go and check that out?"

1

Anger will blur the mind into irrational thinking

"Do you want to?" She wasn't asking a real question. She was puzzled by my inquisitive nature. "It sounded like it came from the principal's office." She paused for a moment and continued, "Yeah, you go and I'll finish loading the students onto the bus."

I walked briskly down the corridor to the main office. As I turned the corner, there was a young teacher holding a sweet-looking African American boy named Jay, who was cussing nonstop. At that moment, Jay broke away from the teacher, grabbed a gray marble tape dispenser, and raised his arm to throw it. I lunged at Jay, knocking the dispenser out of his hands. I grabbed both of his arms and pulled him into the connecting nurse's office,

"Okay, calm down," I said.

"Get off me, motherfucker," was his response.

I said in a calm and reassuring voice, "I will, once you show me that you have calmed yourself."

"Get off me."

"Once again: when you calm down. Now take a deep breath and relax."

Jay complied and his rigid arms went limp. Just as I loosened my grip on his arms, Jay's teacher came into the nurse's office and yelled, "I can't wait to tell your mother how you were . . ." Jay grabbed a pair of eight-inch scissors from the nurse's desk and lunged at the teacher. I managed to grab his right wrist and force the scissors out with my other hand.

"Miss," I said slightly agitated, "I think you should step out and would you please ask Ms. Janis Carpenter to come and give me a hand? Thank you." The young teacher walked out. The whole time Jay was swearing and cursing and his anger was now directed at me. During the training I was instructed to build some kind of rapport with the acting-out child. I never had a chance to. It became important to have a second person there to help in what was turning into a full restraint. Jay was kicking and trying to bite me, so I lifted my weight onto his shoulders, forcing him to the ground. Ms. Carpenter entered the room.

"Oh . . . it's Jay. What's going on? You seem very angry today," Ms. Carpenter said.

"This is great. The teacher is trained in CPI also. Now she can start to build that needed therapeutic rapport with the student," I thought.

"Fuck you . . . *bitch*," Jay screamed.

Janis's eyes opened wide. She twisted her head slightly to one side in an attempt to bite her tongue. She had handled this kind of stuff before, but you could see her patience was running thin. "That's not nice, Jay. I'm only here to help you."

"I don't need your fucking help, bitch."

"Okay, could someone call his house and have his family pick him up. This could go on all day and this isn't Mr. Allen's or my student," she said.

Fortunately for me, Jay's family lived across the street in the Columbia Point projects. We called for the mother but she sent a sixteen-year-old cousin to get him. The young man stood about five feet eleven and weighed a good 175 pounds. The cousin entered the room.

"Hey, get the fuck off him," he yelled at me.

"I will let him go as soon as you get him to calm down."

The young man was now standing over me, his hands balled into a fist. "I said, get off of him."

I could either get up and knock him onto his backside, and have this little twerp attacking me from behind, or I could stand my ground. I looked up and stared him dead in his eyes. I clenched my teeth and said, "I will let him up when you calm him down."

The sixteen-year-old leaned over and tapped Jay on the shoulder and asked, "Are you going to stop?"

Jay responded, "Yes." I let Jay up. Jay took two steps toward his cousin and then attacked me. I immediately placed him back into the restraint.

"This is why I've been holding onto him. He has been like this since I arrived ten minutes ago," I told the cousin.

"Jay-Jay man, what did you do that for?" the cousin asked.

"I'm going to kill this motherfucker," Jay said.

"No, you're not. Stop talking like that so this dude can let you go. Are you going to stop?"

"Yeah," replied Jay.

"You promise, cuz?"

"Yes!"

"All right, let him up man." I slowly let Jay up and physically handed him to the cousin. The principal, who had three months to retirement, entered the room. Her hands were shaking as she prepared herself to hand over the suspension hearing papers. Apparently this fifth grader had her terrified of him for quite some time.

"Here is Jay's suspension paper. We will need to see his mother tomorrow," the principal said. The cousin took the paperwork and the two of them were escorted to the front door. Both Ms. Carpenter and I closed the doors behind them. We started to walk back to our classroom, which took us past the office area.

"Well, Mr. Allen, you just finished your CPI training and you had your first restraint in the same day," she laughed. She continued, "You did a great job in there. You kept your cool. You kept Jay from hurting himself, as well as others."

"Thanks . . . " In front of us about twenty feet away were Jay and his cousin. "I thought you boys left the building."

"He climbed through the nurse's window," said the cousin.

"And you climbed through with him. I think you boys need to go home."

Jay then reached down to his right side and picked up a brown metal trashcan and threw it at Ms. Carpenter and me. I managed to catch it with one hand and gingerly placed it back on the floor. "I want you to leave and get some help before you get hurt. I'll stall them until you are gone," I quietly said to Ms. Carpenter.

"You be careful," she said.

"What was that? Your aim stinks," I said to Jay, directing his attention toward me.

"Oh yeah." Jay reached into his pockets and pulled out some rocks. This kid is good. Jay whipped a rock right at my head. Trying to play it cool, I leaned only my head to the left and the rock flew over my right shoulder.

"See?" I said as I slowly started to back up. Another rock then another whipped by me, as I maneuvered myself out of harm's way. As I looked over my shoulder, I noticed that the hallway was totally clear of innocent people and I ran. Yes, I ran from a rock-throwing delinquent fifth grader bent on doing me harm. Meanwhile, the boys chased me down the hall. I went through the gray doors, the kind with the safety glass, and stopped and waited as I blocked the door with my foot. The two cousins came through and saw me waiting on the other side.

Jay said, "Whatcha gonna do now?" He then whipped his last rock at the glass. It hit so hard it rebounded down the opposite end of the hallway.

"I'm waiting for you to run out of rocks!" I flung the door open and reached for the little brat. The two boys turned and ran out the building.

The next day, the suspension hearing was held. I was asked to be there as was my supervisor who had trained me in CPI. In an inconsiderate, disrespectful tone, the mother began yelling and pointing at me. "Who is this boy who was putting his hands on my son? I'll reach across this table and kick your ass."

My supervisor responded for me, "First of all, this is one of my people, and I am the one who trained him in the procedure he used yesterday. Secondly, miss, if you threaten him again, I will have these police officers escort you out and we will file charges of assault on you. Now, do you understand the expectation of how you need to conduct yourself?"

The woman glared at me and responded with a yes.

My supervisor directed me to describe the details of the story. When I was done the mother said, "I want my son out of this school."

There were strange smiles on the faces of my supervisor and the principal, looks I didn't understand until much later. My boss then said, "I have a perfect school for your son. This school specializes in working with students who act out like Jay does."

The mother said, "I don't care where it is. I just want him out of here." The woman was handed paperwork that she eagerly signed. She stood up and then was escorted out of the building by the school police.

After she left, my boss just started to laugh out loud.

"What did I miss?" I asked.

"She is so angry. She didn't realize that she just she signed her son into a school where he will be restrained every time he acts out physically," said my supervisor.

When this fifth grader attacked others, he was only attacking himself. For me, personal challenges recurred, forcing me to deal with them and signaling my next step toward personal growth and development.

POUND CAKE

*A child bent on revenge will dredge a canyon
that your voice will get lost in.*

I pride myself in having decent working relationships with other teachers. To be able to be the boss while balancing a social life with them makes my work with the teachers fun. One Saturday evening I went out with two teachers and two social workers to a club in Harvard Square. The place was very upbeat and the atmosphere inspired us to act like joyous children. It was a wonderful evening until I saw her. It was Shirlen, a student I had in my first year of teaching graphic arts . . . a student I had not seen since her last day in my class eight years ago . . .

I was taking attendance and suddenly I had a fourteen-year-old girl wearing a white T-shirt and blue jeans standing in front of me. *I know this opaque piece of glass knows I can't take attendance with her standing in front of me,* I thought. As I looked up, only pausing to keep myself calm, I noticed two fully wrapped condoms hanging from her ear lobes, like ornaments you might see in a female strip bar.

"Please remove those from your ears," I said.

She responded by saying, "I'm only trying to promote safe sex."

9

"Oh really," I said. "I know this is graphic art, but we don't express ourselves graphically that way in school. So please remove those from your ears."

"For you, Mr. Allen, I will remove them," she said in a soft, tender voice.

"No, you will just remove them," I informed her.

Slowly each earring came out with each condom it held in place. Shirlen laid each one slowly on the edge of my desk as if to say, "Now, are you satisfied?"

I finished attendance and proceeded to the front of my steel gray desk. Needless to say, the child had not moved, but at least the additions to the earrings were gone. As I arrived at my destination, I heard, "Ooh, she has a pad in her pocket."

Shirlen whipped her backside halfway around and began tapping on the top of the feminine hygiene pad, which was protruding halfway out her right back pocket, and said, "This isn't mine," as she scowled her face.

"Listen, don't you have any scruples?"

In a panicky tone, "This isn't *mine*."

At this point, Shirlen grabbed her crotch and thrust it forward, saying, "Do you see any padding here?" The class began to laugh at her obvious attempt to shock me.

Between clenched teeth I said, "Get outside."

I spent the next two minutes outside the classroom giving the girl etiquette lessons. She nodded her head and gave the standard lip service of how she meant no offense and how it wouldn't happen again.

After we headed back into the classroom, I resumed teaching and Shirlen took her normal seat in the back of the class.

While helping one of the students with his assignment, I noticed faint giggles and growing chatter in the back of the room. As I slowly turned to see what was going on, there was Shirlen in all of her glory, her girlfriends sitting around her with their eyes glazed over, listening to her describe what she did to Johnny the night before.

"I was on top of him, grinding the shit out of him like this," she said.

Shirlen began to demonstrate to her friends. Her hands covered the sides of her head just above her ears, her eyes closed, and her hips gyrated.

"What are you doing?!" I asked in a harsh tone.

Just as quickly and just as harshly, she pointed her index finger at me and said, "Aw Mr. Allen, you *knows* you want some of this cake!"

"Out! Out! Out!"

I've told that story publicly many times. Each time I've been asked why I got so upset with Shirlen, I respond that I simply wasn't going to give anybody the chance to ask me what I did that caused her to say that to me. I learned quickly that it is always important to protect yourself from any potential or imminent threat, or any appearance of impropriety. I wanted her out my classroom permanently.

Four years later, in another middle school, I watched a fellow teacher fail to watch his own back. I had a class up the hall from this teacher. I was teaching computer-aided design and he was teaching woodworking. He kept two seventh grade girls after school for detention one Tuesday afternoon. One was an African American from Dorchester and the other was a white special education student from South Boston. Tanisha, the girl from Dorchester, was a royal pain that day, and other girl, Samantha, was her accomplice. The two of them were running around the woodworking benches, screaming and throwing wood chips at each other. During the detention, the teacher left the room to contact the girls' homes to let their parents know why he was keeping the girls after school. After the girls served their hour detention, the girls were sent home.

The next day, Samantha came to school with her mother ablaze. She wanted the head of the teacher who was feeling all over her daughter's breast while she was in detention. The parent from the Old Colony projects filed a report with the Boston Public Schools and a formal hearing was scheduled for Friday morning. During that whole week, the teacher was ridiculed by his peers and looked on with suspecting eyes. His nerves were shot. He came to me and said he didn't do it. If no one believed him, and these allegations weren't dropped, what use would he be to his wife and five kids?

The meeting was very hot, with accusations flying and potential penalties and outcomes being foretold. For some reason, the mother asked the daughter, "Explain what happened. How do you know mister was touching all over you?"

Samantha responded, "Because Tanisha told me so."

During the time the teacher was out of the classroom calling the parents, Tanisha brainwashed the special needs child into thinking that she was sexually assaulted. Tanisha kept repeating to Samantha, "How can you let mister feel all over your breast like that. Didn't you feel his hand crawl up your shirt?"

The parent apologized to the teacher. It scares me to think that a teacher's career would have been destroyed if that parent didn't ask the right question at the right time.

These incidents proved three things:

1. Every teacher and administrator must develop his or her own survival kit.

2. Even a seventh grader knows about revenge.

3. Above all, it is crucial to develop a distaste for "pound cake" in all its varieties.

In August 1997, I accepted a promotion to assistant headmaster in one of the high schools in the city of Boston. This was a great opportunity for me. I was placed in charge of the math department, science department, and the school's $5 million budget. I also oversaw the lead teacher program in the school, along with my own discipline load.

Later in the year during an administrative needs assessment meeting, which included the headmaster, three assistant headmasters, the bilingual department head, and the special needs department head, it was determined that a new curriculum needed to be developed. (This meeting was necessitated because of an upcoming high school accreditation and the results of the Stanford 9 test.) It was a prime opportunity because the school was about to undergo a $31 million renovation. I suggested that the new curriculum emphasize basic skills instruction and cognitive skills development to raise test scores in math and English. The team agreed and we decided to work on improving student achievement by developing a small learning community at a separate site with a low student-to-teacher ratio; this site would become known as the Annex.

One of the hottest topics of the meeting was, Who was going to be put in charge of this Annex? I admit that I didn't want it. I had taught at the middle school level for seven years, and administering the Annex would be like two years in purgatory. But I was the right person for the job and I agreed to take on the responsibility—if I would be allowed to do it my way. I wanted complete autonomy to design a small school that would work under a holistic vision of education: to educate the whole child beyond standard academics. My goal was to have all students learn how they fit in the world around them and how their academics are not a series of individual courses but an aggregate of formulated ideas.

During the meeting the secretary entered the room. "I'm sorry to interrupt, but you guys need to get to room 201. A student says there is a fight. I've already requested school police to go to that room."

We stood up, looking at each other to figure out who would go first. Then one of the other assistant headmasters said, "It's your classroom, Mr. Allen." I shut my file and took a slow, deep breath, trying to settle my stomach, and then proceeded to lead the way. By the time we power walked down the beige and brown hall, the school police officers had already pulled the students apart. One of my boys (called D) had facial injuries. His eyes were puffed out. His nose was dripping blood and his speech was incoherent. The other young man, Troy, huffed and puffed but showed no marks on his body.

13

"What happened?" I asked the teacher who was standing outside of the classroom.

She pointed at Troy. "He tried to kill that boy. He walked into my classroom and I asked him if I could help him. He said no, so I asked him to leave. As I walked over to him, he shoved a metal chair into me, tripping me up. He then jumped up onto the desk and began to pound on D's head. Troy was screaming, 'Whatcha gonna say now?'"

"Is all that true, Troy?" I asked.

"Yeah," he responded.

"What would you do that for?" I wanted to know.

"Mr. Allen, you wouldn't understand." There was a hint of sarcasm in his voice.

"Is this part of some sick perverted pleasure?" I asked. Troy did not respond. I was mortified. I haven't seen anyone's face torn up this bad since Thomas Hearns fought Sugar Ray.

"No, no," I said in disgust. "Come into this office and explain this to me." As Troy was escorted to the upper office, school police grabbed his arms and placed handcuffs around his wrists.

"Do they have to do that, Mr. Allen?" His sarcastic voice turned to panic.

"It's called an assault and battery, son." When we reached the small office, I pointed to a wooden chair and continued, "Have a seat here. Now, explain this to me."

"You won't understand." He blinked and began to gaze around the room as if he were looking for a way to escape.

"Listen, you better come up with something really good."

"Okay. He's been sexually harassing me," blurting out his words to show the world the injustice that had taken place.

"How do you figure that?" I asked in extreme disbelief.

He looked down at his feet and began to tremble. "Every day for the last week, D has been coming up to me telling me how cute my ass is. I kept telling him, I'm not like that and to leave me alone. Today, while I was in the bathroom taking a pee, he walked up behind me and said he can't wait to get a hold of my ass and then he grabbed me. All of the dudes in the bathroom started laughing." He then looked me dead in my eyes and continued, "That shit is embarrassing, Mr. Allen. You don't understand; I *had to* kick his ass. I don't want them thinking I'm like that."

"Listen, did you ask any of us to help you before it went this far?" I questioned.

"That shit is embarrassing, Mr. Allen. I can't just walk up to you and tell you that some dude wants me like that. If it was a girl, I could handle that. But this is a dude. You're a man. You know what it is I'm talking about. Tell me you wouldn't have kicked his ass. Tell me," he pleaded.

I couldn't answer.

In May 1998, the Annex project was started. Teachers who volunteered for the ninth grade cluster were provided with a substitute and spent an all-day professional development session discussing and designing a curriculum that was viewed as holistic in its approach to educating students. It was my goal that this session would be the start of a supportive environment that fostered trust and teachers' investment in the school. It was considered the official beginning of the high school restructuring plan that included activities directed at changing teachers' instructional methods rather than students' behavior.

The first accomplishment of the six-hour session was the planning day schedule, which provided common planning time for teachers. Every eleventh day, students would be released an hour and a half early. The planning day was intended to lead to a supportive climate. The group of teachers met to look at student achievement and their own teaching skills.

The second accomplishment was establishing a thematic approach to learning for the ninth grade students at the school. Each twelve-week term the curriculum was arranged around a theme. Around these themes interdisciplinary lessons were structured. A different component was taught in each subject area, and in this way all classes were webbed together. For example, during the third term, students would study "wisdom, humanity and you" (WHY). In science, students would study light and sound and how they affect humanity while gaining the prerequisite skills (Sharma 1979) necessary for an upcoming technology education class. In technology, the class would take that learning process a step further by developing a fiber-optics telephone. The English department chose literature that focused on friendship and related it to the WHY theme, for example, *Of Mice and Men, Night,* and *I Know Why the Cage Bird Sings.*

The Annex was envisioned as a working laboratory that would serve as a model of a smaller learning community for restructuring the school. The Annex would consist of 250 students, fifteen teachers, and one administrator. The electives for the first year would consist of music, army JROTC, and computers. Schoolwide, the student-to-teacher ratio was to be 15 to 1. The actual class sizes would run 19 to 1, after figuring in a professional development period for teachers and an administrative period. Features of this small learning community included:

- A focus on teacher teamwork and involvement

- A plan to increase parent involvement

- A built-in common faculty planning time

- An innovative flexible class schedule

- A guest speaker series and assemblies

- Field trips linked to the curriculum

- A focus on students' math and science skills with an emphasis on skill application via engaging students in portfolio evaluations, critical thinking, cognitive development exercises, and problem solving

- A student recognition program

- A faculty advising/mentoring program

- Collaborative workshops between Annex and main building teachers for shared professional development opportunities.

These innovations were implemented in September 1998 and continued more than two years until the two sites were merged and the Annex practices were adopted schoolwide. The school chose these elements based on the following criteria: All members of the school community would take ownership of these practices. All faculty members would be part of the curricular development and would accept responsibility for the school and its charge to educate its student body. Under the old model, teachers did not appear to care if the students learned. I wanted teachers who were invested in the program, since I was going to offer unique opportunities for teachers to demonstrate their creativity.

In my heart, I knew one thing would always remain true and would make or break the school: there would be a focus on both teamwork and relationships. I found through my discussions with the teachers that schools typically alienate students and I wanted a school that promoted teamwork and built positive relationships between teachers and students. Our teachers differed in methods and personal style, but they explicitly and implicitly modeled and conveyed to students positive behavioral and interpersonal relationship norms. These ideas would be empowering and would help build that necessary sense of community.

We wanted a hands-on curriculum that would engage our students. Through our observations, we saw students who were bored with school. We believed that if we could make learning interesting and relevant to their lives, our students would develop a positive attitude about their education. My strong belief that students should be assessed by means other than a test led me to push for the use of portfolios.

Additionally, our current school had poor parent attendance during our mandated open houses; sometimes only 10 percent of our parents would attend. Our goal was to increase parental involvement to a minimum of 35 percent.

I have offered this background information to provide a context for understanding some of the complex situations that arose in this alternative setting, which I describe in following chapters.

APRIL FOOLS, 1999

The press is not your friend.

Eight years have passed since my encounter with Shirlen. Many other moments in my teaching career also stand out, but that first encounter with Shirlen is the most notable. Since that time, I have watched the birth of my children, divorced my first wife, and completed two more college degrees. I would love to think that in retrospect my past experiences have played a small role in who I have become and in how I respond to difficult situations. But in fact, past experiences have played a large role in my reactions and have taught me the boundaries of my patience.

My past, especially my divorce from my first wife, has made me a stronger person. I had met Jawanna through friends. This was a woman who turned out to have three other identities: Jawanna Liealot, Jawanna Cheatalot, and Jawanna Berippinyouoff with two provable social security numbers. Sometimes I wish I had never met her. But when I think about the types of roles I've had as an administrator in a major school in the city, in a twisted way I have to thank my ex-wife for making me a very self-assured, thick-skinned man. Someone once told me, "You can't be an administrator unless you have the skin of an alligator." He was right.

I'm in my first fight with the press. Outside of my school are trucks belonging to three local television stations and one cable station. My school is right next door to Fenway Park, and such media attention is usually reserved for baseball. Like a little child, I've been hiding behind pillars and darting behind overly large friends. It helps that the press doesn't know what I look like. I keep my phone number unpublished, and I definitely don't look like your typical school administrator.

It all started when Mr. Martin came to the Annex and forcefully requested an interview with me. My substitute secretary entered my office looking very upset. "Mr. Allen, I have this Martin guy outside. He says he is a reporter from the *Boston Herald* and he wants to talk to you about Sam Coles."

"Please tell Mr. Martin I am busy and that there isn't any story here for him. If he would like to return later to attend our multicultural fair, he would be welcomed. It is a great humanistic story." The secretary left to deliver the message and returned quickly.

"First of all, he is very rude and pushy. He says that he will write the story with or without you and he is submitting it at the end of the day."

"Tell Mr. Martin that is fine. If he wants more information, he can speak with the communications office in town."

Sam was stopped outside my office because I had received four complaints from students that he had put itching powder on them. This wouldn't normally be a big deal but this time one of them broke out in hives. Sam was searched but nothing was found. He was sent home with a suspension hearing letter.

The next day, Sam arrived at school without a parent or guardian and was immediately made to call home. To say that it was literally painful to talk to his parents is an understatement. The grandmother, who wore a hearing aid, had a tendency to scream into the phone. When I engaged her in conversation, I would hold the phone two feet away from my right ear. Sometimes I would place the receiver on the desk and walk around the room. The volume was so piercing that she could be heard clearly across the room. The grandmother began her loud-pitched, British-accented bravado with, "Sam said he didn't do it."

The three-minute conversation with the grandmother ended with her being told that she must come in the next day at 8:30 A.M. for the suspension hearing and that Sam was being sent home for the rest of the day.

I then received a phone call from Sam's mother stating she was going to the superintendent and both of them would be at the meeting.

Yeah, right, I thought.

Wait a minute. She's coming? Karen Coles is coming here? Oh God, please help me. The last time I spoke to this woman she said, "I don't care what he hears about the main building; he's at the Annex. Sam knows. I will come up there; I'll punch him in the face. I will beat the shit out of him. I'll come up there and pull his pants down in front of everyone and beat him."

In this job, instinct plays a large role. This time it said, Have someone with you. Don't do this meeting alone with this woman.

The next morning Sam and his mom, a biracial woman with light brown hair, arrived at 7:55 A.M. She glared at me as I walked by. I could understand her being upset at Sam, but Ms. Coles was directing her anger at me. So I ignored her for five minutes hoping that she would cool off. I called both of them into my office, and right behind them was Mary, school security.

Ms. Coles began by stating her advocate wasn't present.

I told her, "We can wait. The official start time is 8:30 A.M. and I will begin at that time, with or without the advocate."

Rolling her eyes, Ms. Coles said I could begin, but when the advocate got to the meeting, she was going to object to everything.

During the meeting, Sam blamed me for all of his problems. Both he and his mother tried to change the subject several times. I kept going back to why we were having a suspension hearing. When he heard the decision, Sam began to cry. In the middle of one of his

21

sentences, his mother rose out of her seat like it was on fire. She took one elongated step toward Sam, and from way down south and with an immense authority, launched her assault, hitting Sam palm first, frontal, knocking his head back. As he came forward, he was met with another blow to the face.

I leaned forward in the direction of Ms. Coles and said, "I wouldn't do that in my office."

Ms. Coles sat down. There was an uncomfortable moment of silence.

I thought to myself, *I'm a mandated reporter. Do I file a 51A?* According to Massachusetts General Laws, chapter 119, section 51A, a mandated reporter is someone

> who, in his professional [judgment] shall have reasonable cause to believe that a child under the age of eighteen years is suffering physical or emotional injury resulting from abuse inflicted upon him which causes harm or substantial risk of harm to the child's health or welfare including sexual abuse, or from neglect, including malnutrition, or who is determined to be physically dependent upon an addictive drug at birth, shall immediately report such condition to the department by oral communication and by making a written report within forty-eight hours after such oral communication.

No. Just get them out of my space. Do it after they leave. But what happens when the Department of Social Services (DSS) asks me why I let him go home with the mother? Deal with that later.

"Sam is suspended for two days." Again to myself, *There's blood coming from his nose, damn.*

"Here Sam, use this for your nose." I leaned over my desk, gesturing with the white tissue to get Sam to use it. Ms. Coles jumped up, snatched the tissue out of my hand, and threw it into the trash.

"He doesn't need it! He knows I don't put up with that fucking shit."

Mary and I looked at each other as if to say, "Do you believe this?"

Ms. Coles said coldly, "Call 911."

Puzzled, I responded, "Call 911?"

"Yes," she said. "If you're accusing Sam of an assault and battery and having an illegal substance, whatever that is, then call 911."

"Sam did something wrong and we will handle it internally. But he didn't do anything that requires me to call 911."

Sam's mother said it again just as heartlessly as before, and without a hint of remorse. "I want you to call 911."

"Sam didn't do anything," I insisted.

Callously Ms. Coles said, "I don't want him anymore, I want you to call 911."

Firmly and emotionlessly I said, "Are you *sure* you want me to call 911?"

Ms. Coles was aggravated. "Yes, I want you to call 911."

Beep, beep, beep.

At this point Ms. Coles started to leave.

"Where are you going?"

"They're coming to take him, I don't need to be here."

"Wait, you asked me to call them, so they are going to want to ask you some questions. I called at your behest."

Within two minutes, I had five Boston police officers in my office. After telling them the story, I told them I was very concerned with the blood coming out of Sam's nose, and the blood on his hand and shirt.

The police officer walked over to Sam and asked him if he understood that what he did was wrong.

Sam responded with a yes.

He then asked Sam if he would ever make that mistake again.

Sam said no.

The officer then turned around and said, "Ms. Coles, I'm placing you under arrest for assault and battery on a minor."

As Ms. Coles was taken to the police station, she kept repeating, "I don't want him any more."

One week later, the manhunt began. No comment. No comment.

I've had time to reflect on that day and the events that followed and I wish I had done a few things differently. First, I should have just told Ms. Coles that if I called 911 she was the one who would be arrested. The adversity was a challenge and a great character-building experience for me. But I don't know if my actions had a greater positive or negative effect on Sam. There were very few issues with him after this incident. His mother never acted out in school again.

Second, I wish I had soft jazz or classical music playing in the background (a practice I keep up now). I find this calms the parents and helps diffuse what can be a hot situation. I've had parents stop in the middle of their fit to ask about the artist performing that particular piece.

Third, I would have dealt with the press myself instead of having my secretary deliver the message. Not speaking to a reporter is the same as saying no comment. In today's climate, "no comment" is looked on as a sign of guilt. Regardless if I was trying to keep Sam safe and keep his name out of the papers, my lack of response to the press would be suspect. I thought at the time that if I didn't talk to them, then there wasn't a story to tell. It was the wrong thought. The reporter was going to make a story whether I helped or not. I should have framed my response with concerns in the context of what's in the best interest of the child.

Additional editorial articles attempted to perpetuate the situation by adding their unfounded point of view. The authors of those articles tried to say that the incident made it "a tough road for parents" when they want to discipline their children. The facts are that Sam was not yelling or swearing at me that day. Sam was crying. Karen Coles was frustrated at the fact that her son was caught and was being served the punishment that was due, but what was not due was a bloody nose. In my years before and my years after this April Fools Day, I have never had another parent draw blood in my presence. If it ever becomes necessary, I'll be the first person to hand a parent a belt. It is unfortunate when any child cannot be reasoned with. It is a horrible situation when a student verbally and physically refuses to follow the rules, forcing the adult to respond even more forcefully. But the kind of beating that Sam received was not discipline, it was abuse, and Karen Coles suffered the consequences of her actions. Karen Coles's scheme to rid herself of her son that day backfired. Hopefully, the stupidity of those who went looking for a story backfired too. If anything good came out of those articles, it would be that abusive parents are thinking carefully about what is due.

All things happen for a reason. In my first marriage, I initially thought the joke was on me, but I was being toughened to meet crises later in life. Ms. Coles thought the onus was on Sam, but it was on her—to prepare herself for real motherhood before she and her son parted company.

LITTLE BAGS OF CHEEBA

"Mr. Allen, Wesley arrived at the science museum an hour and a half late," said one of my teachers.

"Did he say why?"

"There shouldn't have been a reason. We all left the school at the same time," the teacher said.

"Oh!" I mused.

Forty-five minutes later, Wesley arrived at school with his entourage. Wesley was what you would call a pretty boy. The girls loved him. He came to school dressed in the latest fashions: Timberland boots, baggy jeans, and a matching du rag.

"Wesley, come here, please." Wesley slowly strutted over to me. "It was brought to my attention that you arrived late to the field trip yesterday. Would you like to tell me why?"

As Wesley spoke, the odor from his mouth, which seemed to stem from his bowels, numbed my eyes. My involuntary action to cover my mouth and nose halted Wesley's speech.

"Wesley, you stink! Have you been smoking marijuana?"

Peer to peer pressure can transform the meek into an outlaw regime.

With an incongruous grin Wesley said, "Why yes, Mr. Allen."

To myself, *This boy is so stoned, he has no clue as to what he has just admitted.*

"Wesley, step over here to Officer Hank Simmons." I wanted a second opinion before doing what I had to do.

Wesley followed me over to the officer. "Simmons, do you smell anything?" I asked.

"I smell a *strong* odor of marijuana," he said.

"Okay, Wesley into my office please."

After entering my office, I asked Wesley for his book bag, so it could be searched.

"You can search my bag. I don't have anything to hide."

"Good, then you have nothing to worry about." The search began by checking each pocket of the black backpack. I continued, "Is there anything in these pockets I need to be concerned about?"

Wesley answered, "No. Like what?"

"A gun, a knife, a hypodermic needle."

"No."

I slowly opened the main compartment. Nothing there but a light gray bag.

"That's my Walkman," Wesley said in a suspicious voice.

"Oh." To myself, *Why did he have to tell me that? Something is wrong.* I proceeded to unzip the bag.

"Oh my . . . Hank." I could not believe what I was seeing.

"What?" Asked Hank.

"Look." I motioned, further opening the bag in his direction.

"Uh-oh . . ."

There before my eyes were fourteen bags of what appeared to be marijuana, all neatly wrapped in plastic Saran Wrap balls.

"Wesley, have you been selling marijuana in my school?" I inquired.

"Nah, Mr. A., just outside. Ten dollars a bag." He said nonchalantly.

"For what?" I just wanted to know.

"I was helping out one of my peeps," he said, expecting me to understand.

"Your peeps?"

Wesley nodded as he said, "Yeah."

"Are your peeps going to help you get out of jail? Empty out your pockets," I demanded.

Slowly Wesley emptied his left pocket. Nothing. I tapped the outside of his black jeans pocket. "What is that?"

I got no response from Wesley.

"Pull the whites all the way out." Wesley reached in and began to pull the white lining of his pockets out of his pants. One bag of Mary Jane. "Pull them right out." Two more bags. "Wesley is carrying a full store up in there. It's time to start making some phone calls."

Wesley was arrested by school police and transported to the district for booking.

Expulsion hearing:

The parent arrived with her lawyer. The first thing Wesley's mother said to me was, "Did you read Wesley his rights?"

I responded, "I'm not a police officer."

"You should have read him his rights," she insisted.

Actually the laws had changed that year. Not only are the police now expected to read him his rights, but I am supposed to inform him of them also.

During the expulsion hearing the parent was told that she has a right to appeal the disciplinary action within ten days. Wesley's mother appealed the case to the ombudsman in the superintendent's office and the expulsion was almost turned down. Wesley was still expelled because under our rules he can be expelled if convicted of committing a felony, which he was.

Someone carrying seventeen bags of marijuana makes for an easy case to prove intent to distribute on school grounds. A strong case, like this one, can be blown if the administrator fails to keep up with the legal and political landscape. Albert Einstein said, "The only source of knowledge is experience." I will add that the knowledge must be wrapped in a foundation rich in text.

Why do parents enable their children to continue to act inappropriately? Festinger would describe this situation as a prime example of cognitive dissonance. This is a tendency for an individual to seek consistency among their cognitions (beliefs, opinions). To quote Leon Festinger (1957), "When there is an inconsistency between attitudes or behaviors (dissonance), something must change to eliminate the dissonance. In the case of a discrepancy between attitudes and behavior, it is most likely that the attitude will change to accommodate the behavior."

I understand that parents feel obligated to protect their children. I'm a parent; I know that urge too well. Still, I believe that it is better for children to learn their lesson while they are young, instead of doing serious time as adults.

As the biblical saying goes, "Spare the rod and spoil the child." The "little bags of Cheeba" have already spoiled our children. In our reluctance to take up the rod of chastisement or correction, we have compounded the problems of our youth, for we have robbed them of their moral compass. It is our responsibility as administrators to place more value on the lives of our students, no matter how difficult the outcome.

A BOY NAMED TYREE

I watched a stocky young man named Tyree as he entered the school at the beginning of the day. I could tell he was upset and he seemed to be looking for answers. When he saw me, he quickened his pace to ensure his interception.

Bursting with rage and on the verge of a torrent of words he began, "Yo, Mr. Allen, we need to talk."

"Come on in, Tyree. What's going on?"

"Why did you tell everyone my business?"

"Whoa, stop!" I interrupted, "What are you talking about?"

"Did you talk to the press or anybody about me?"

"No. Now please start from the beginning. I have no idea what you're talking about."

"My boys, my own boys are out to get me. They think I'm a snitch. I didn't say nothing. Nothing and now they want me dead, yo. I ain't safe nowhere. I can't walk nowhere. Someone gonna be dead this summer, yo."

"Tyree, slow down and start from the beginning," I begged.

"That lieutenant sold me out. My boy in prison was reading a magazine and he read it all. We were sitting around chillin' with the

You can add basil, you can add thyme, but if the pot is full of shit when you start, it is full of bullshit when you're done!

rest of the gang, talking with my boy on the speakerphone. Then he broke out with 'Tyree is a snitch you all.' I'm sitting there saying, what is you talking about, and he starts reading my business. They all start staring at me, talking about a beat down. I'd tried telling them that it wasn't me, but they wouldn't believe me. I just jetted. They want me dead, yo."

"Lieutenant, the one I requested to help you, caused this predicament?" I asked in disbelief.

"Yeah." Tyree said, shaking his head and staring hopelessly at his feet. "They already beat my brother down."

"What magazine?"

"I think it was *Boston Magazine*."

"Well, let's get a copy."

After a couple of phone calls, a faxed copy of the article arrived.

"Oh my; this is a.k.a. Tyree." What was the lieutenant thinking? He tagged Tyree in every possible way. His gang association, the mark on his face, and how he got that mark on his face. He described Tyree's foster mother's dialect and what neighborhood she is from. He must have lost his mind or believed he is from Zion if he thinks that by changing this young man's name, it would make Tyree safe. He sold this boy out for a piece of publicity. He used him for a "puff piece."

Boston Magazine quoted other cops in speaking about the lieutenant as saying, "'Lieutenant' is the man with the juice, the human weatherman can just about pinpoint what storm clouds will rumble out of which schools and spill into the street."

It seems this school is only rumbling because of his big mouth. What an asshole, I thought.

"Tyree, we will do what we can to make you safe. We will also make some phone calls to the lieutenant to get some answers."

Without any hesitation Tyree snapped, "I don't want to talk to him."

"You should. You have every right to know why he did what he did." Tyree, after a lot of persuading, finally agreed to meet with the lieutenant.

A few days later there was a meeting between Tyree, the lieutenant, Boston police, the school police, and myself.

The lieutenant immediately attempted to take the meeting over, hoping to set the tone. "I know this is going to be hard for you to hear, Tyree, but sometimes this stuff happens for the best."

Tyree jumped up and said the first two words that were in my mind with the authority of Thor and the true passion that drives us, "Fuck you!" He then continued, "I'm not listening to this *bullshit*," pointing at the lieutenant.

I called out to him, "Tyree, wait a minute."

"Naw, fuck him!" he said as he left my office.

I looked at the lieutenant with the hate a father gives to any man who has hurt his child. "I don't know what you were thinking, but he isn't going to listen to that crap. As far as he is concerned you sold him out and he wants to know why."

Just as arrogant as he was when he entered the office, the lieutenant said, "Well, let's look at the facts. He has always been in a bad situation . . ."

I interrupted, "Does that mean you have to make a bad situation worse? At least before you intervened, he had one safe way home. Now he has no way home. Every gang wants his *ass*, including his own. Not only have you endangered Tyree, you have endangered every student in this school. You have made them potential victims of a drive-by shooting. You know those bullets don't have any specific name on them when they begin to fly. You have also put my life and my faculty's lives in danger, and quite frankly, you have managed to piss me off."

At this point the Boston police officer interrupted and said, "What do you want to happen?"

"I want Tyree moved to a safe location. I want Tyree's foster family moved to a safe location. And I want Boston police posted on duty outside of the school fifteen minutes before and after school."

"We will provide you with a patrol officer and look into your first two requests. We can definitely have Tyree moved, but I don't know about the mother. Anything else?"

"For now, that will do; but if I don't see action within the next twenty-four hours, you, lieutenant, will have a problem."

Starting the next day, there was a constant police presence outside of the school. Tyree was moved to a new foster home. Unfortunately the original foster family was not moved, but they did not have any other problems from the gang. Two years later Tyree was seen walking through the streets of Boston. A teacher who spoke with him said he looked fairly well. She said that Tyree told her that he was still trying to finish school by getting his GED.

Although this is a boy named Tyree, how many other boys' futures have been bartered for fifteen minutes of fame, which might as well be thirty pieces of silver. It is the job of all of us to take the weight of the bull off the backs of our children and point them in the direction of a bright future, equipped with the tools to succeed.

YOU JUST DON'T KNOW

*Eye contact can speak the word that words themselves
are unable to accurately communicate.*

This is my second year at the Annex, and those of us here have had our fair share of ups and downs. What has made us strong is our commitment to work together to help these kids achieve. We developed the STOMPERS program (Student of the Month, Perfect Attendance Student). We started the program at the beginning of the year with just twelve students. We are now more than halfway through the year and our enrollment has grown to 220. Having large numbers going on field trips creates its own issues.

It never seems to fail, while you are dealing with one issue, another seems to arise. Officer Mercer and I were talking when a huge eruption happened in one of the classrooms. You could hear desks and chairs being thrown across the room, and the eerie sound they made as they screeched across the floor permeated the halls and induced fear. The screams were similar to those you hear on television, like screams by a woman witnessing a murder in progress. Both of us ran into the room to stop the catfight. Officer Mercer circled around to the left, and I to the right. He grabbed Lisa and I grabbed Neil Cox. A boy–girl fight.

Immediately Officer Mercer asked, "All I want to know is who was screaming like that?"

In unison, the class answered, "Neil." Neil Cox came to us from another state and had spent many years in juvenile centers. Neil stood five feet eleven inches and was proud that he weighed 105 pounds. He tried to appear secure in his femininity by wearing women's black boots.

Eye contact can speak the word that words themselves are unable to accurately communicate. Officer Mercer and I said the unspoken words like no other that day. After interviewing each student and sending Neil to the school nurse for the scratches he received, both students were sent home and both students were told not to return to school unless their parent or guardian accompanied them.

Meanwhile, another student's mother was waiting for me.

"Mr. Allen, I've been waiting for you for twenty minutes," she said.

"I'm sorry, miss, but as you can see I had an emergency to take care of. You are?"

"I'm Hector's mother."

"Yes, I'm glad you could make it to school. Please step into my office. Officer Mercer, would you like to join us please?" Mercer slowly walked over and joined our small circle. "Miss, I asked you to come in for a conference because we are concerned about Hector's behavior. He has been skipping school, and I have received several reports that he has threatened to beat up some students."

Mercer interjected, "I seen him running out the side door during lunch time yesterday."

The mother barked, "No, that's not my Hector. You . . . you just don't like my Hector. That why you say such nasty things about him."

"Excuse me?" I said.

Her tone angered and her Spanish accent thickened and as she accentuated her points her gestures flared. "You don't give him a fair chance. You just want to kick him out. Hector is a good boy, a good boy," she said as she pounded her fist into her hand.

"Miss, no one wants to or has ever kicked him out. Hector got up and walked out of this school repeatedly *on his own*. Look at his classroom attendance record. He has skipped out of school every day at 11:30 for over a week. So Hector's skipping has nothing to do with me. Now because of Hector's skipping, I'm going to give him an in-school suspension with me all day tomorrow."

The short, dark-haired Hispanic mom nodded her head and told her son to be in my office the next day.

"Hey Mr. Allen, I've been looking for Hector today to make sure he showed up to your office, but I haven't seen him. I think he's skipping again."

"Thanks, Mercer. I'll let you tell his mom; her son isn't being a good boy."

"Why? So she can blame me for her son's problems?"

"That's right! Blame the black man." Mercer shook his head. I continued, "Seriously, I will call her and let her know. I will also let her know that he has now doubled his detention time, for failure to show."

Ms. Norma Cox has finally arrived and has sat in front of me. She is an older woman with salt-and-pepper hair. She rocks back and forth slowly as she rubs her knees and gingerly caresses the curl of her cane. She is in obvious pain. Her knees are swollen from years of overuse; it is the kind of edema that comes with arthritis. Ms. Cox is the kind grandmother type who has chosen to care for one of her grandchildren. Neither of Neil's parents is capable of taking care of him.

"You just don't know what the boy is putting me through," Norma sighed.

"Well, Ms. Cox, I remember what you told me the last time we met. So what is Neil up to this time?"

There was a slow and heavy pause. Norma, who was still nervously holding her cane, slowly peered around to see if anyone had entered the room unnoticed. She looked down and then up at me, with eyes that begged not to tell the information she was about to give.

"I walked into the room and there is Neil putting on his lip-stick."

Between each line she'd looked at me with those grandmotherly eyes to see if I understood or to see what my response would be.

To myself, *Did I hear her right?*

She continued, "Then he starts to put his weave in his hair."

·Again to myself, *Damn, I heard her right. Don't laugh, don't smile. Put on one of those serious, concerned faces.* Part of me wanted to laugh, but those eyes. I looked at her and she had that serious look on her face and within those eyes, the kind of look that grandmothers have when their grandchildren aren't doing what they expect them to.

"I asked him, baby what are you doing? And he says to me, 'Grandma, I'm going out to make some money.' You know, Mr. Allen. I had to tell him that he didn't have to do that. And he had to ask me, 'Why not?' I had to tell him how much we loved him and he didn't have to disrespect himself like that anymore."

He said, "Grandma, I spent my life locked up in that place and no one ever told me they loved me. They never gave me a hug. They would just hop on my back and do their thing. That's the only love I know. That school is the first time I ever been in a public school that I like . . . And they ain't going to kick me out of my school.

"Mr. Allen, I was surprised that Neil was so attached to the An-nex. Even though he is a pain when he is here, Neil believes that this is his place. I need some help with this boy. I don't know what to do with him," she said as she shook her head.

"Ms. Cox, the school can help you get counseling for Neil. We have counseling interns in the building who can support your grand-son throughout the day. Or if you wish, we can help you make arrangements outside of the building."

"That would be wonderful, Mr. Allen." There was a momentary smile on Ms. Cox's face.

"I'm glad you are able to share this information with me. It gives me a baseline to work with. What I do need from you is to under-stand the school's position. Despite the fact that Neil has all of these issues, his behavior cannot be excused. So I do need to tell you that he is suspended for three days for fighting in the school. I would like to have a mediation meeting with him and the girl when they return."

"That's fine, Mr. Allen."

From the time Neil was eight to his current age of fourteen, he was committed to a residential program for juvenile offenders. For six years, his peers and his care providers raped him. Prior to his committal, his stepfather molested him and then used Neil's acting out as a reason to get him medicated. This boy never had a chance. No amount of antidepressants would ever make him feel normal and secure again—if ever he did feel normal and secure.

Neil's response to his grandmother and his behavior in school should not come as a surprise. Studies have shown that many forms of child abuse can cause physical disorders and have psychological consequences. The National Clearinghouse on Child Abuse and Neglect Information website states:

> Child abuse and neglect have been shown, in some cases, to cause important regions of the brain to fail to form properly, resulting in impaired physical, mental, and emotional development (Perry 2002; Shore 1997). In other cases, the stress of chronic abuse causes a "hyperarousal" response by certain areas of the brain, which may result in hyperactivity, sleep disturbances, and anxiety, as well as increased vulnerability to post-traumatic stress disorder, attention deficit/hyperactivity disorder, conduct disorder, and learning and memory difficulties (Perry 2001; Dallam 2001).

They go on to say that children who are abused and neglected by caretakers often do not form secure attachments to them. These abused connections can lead to later difficulties in relationships with adults and peers. To make the situation worse, the child who is placed in out-of-home care tends to score lower than the general population on measures of cognitive capacity, language development, and academic achievement.

Other studies have found abused and neglected children to be at least 25 percent more likely to experience problems such as delinquency, teen pregnancy, low academic achievement, drug use, and mental health problems (Kelley et al. 1997). Supporting studies indicated that abuse and neglect increased the likelihood of adult criminal behavior by 28 percent and violent crime by thirty percent (Widom and Maxfield 2001).

Many months later (after Neil had served his suspension) I entered a math teacher's classroom. This is not uncommon for me. It is an important part of my role as an administrator to be visible. Being out in the halls and in the classroom brings another level of accountability to the faculty and the students. My initial survey of the room wasn't pleasant. The students were playing music, reading the newspaper, and having general social conversations. It looked like a scene from *Lean on Me* or *Dangerous Minds* before the turning point. The class, including the teacher's facial features, turned to fright. Please understand I have this God-given ability to produce an emotionless stare that can kill a joyous moment.

"Mr. Whop, I thought this was an algebra class."

"Mr. Allen, they don't listen to me. They only listen to you," he said as he scurried to put his newspaper away.

"Sir, if you want to keep your job, you'd better figure out how to get them to listen to you. Just sitting there, reading the paper is not showing high expectations." I swear this guy is the Forrest Gump of teaching. "Stupid is as stupid does."

Meanwhile, most of the students are scurrying to put their papers and radios away. Well, all but one. You could hear his classmates telling him, "Mr. Allen is here, put your stuff away." Officer Mercer enters the room behind me.

Neil begins to talk out loud, holding his paper in front of him as if he were still reading and said, "I don't give a fuck. I want to see him come here and do something about it. I'll fuck him up."

The class gestures and makes the universal sound for "be quiet." "Shhhhhhhhhhh!"

With an appropriate relationship, students can be an administrator's best allies. Students can clue you in to the disposition of the acting-out child. Peer pressure can make an ugly situation calm and workable. As your allies, students can communicate and reinforce the positive standard of behavior. Neil wasn't biting.

"No! You heard me. I'll fuck him up."

In the end it is always the administrator's or teacher's responsibility to pick the best strategy to use. I had to decide whether to ignore or punish Neil's undesirable behavior. Initially I wanted to throw him out of the school, but it dawned on me at that instant that, first, that is what the student wanted and, second, that is what the teacher wanted. And really, it was the teacher's fault this was going on. Linda Albert (1995) in her book *Cooperative Discipline* states that students choose to misbehave to achieve one of four goals: (1) get attention, (2) have some kind of power over a situation, (3) get revenge, and (4) avoid failure. Neil is an extreme case. Typically students try to achieve one goal of misbehavior. I believed Neil was trying to achieve three outcomes. He was trying to get extra attention so that he could be center stage. Neil was on a power trip trying to control the classroom environment to prove that he was in charge of himself and that he was the boss. By getting himself thrown out of school, Neil could avoid the inadequacies that were leading to his continued failure in math.

I turned around and looked at Officer Mercer and said, "Did you hear what Neil said?"

Officer Mercer said, "The part that he said he was going to eff you up?"

"Yes, that part." Officer Mercer and I stared at each other for a moment and our eyes began to water. The laughter began to pour out uncontrollably. We comforted each other as we rested on each other's shoulders. The students began to laugh, saying, "Mr. Allen is laughing. Oh shoot, he just brushed you off. He totally dismissed you. I guess you're not going home early."

Officer Mercer and I closed the door and calmed ourselves. "I don't think he'll make that mistake again," I said. And he never did, at least not with me.

As for Mr. Whop, he didn't take my warning seriously. He continued to teach poorly and made no effort to correct his failings. The teacher was evaluated out of teaching in the high school at the end of the school year.

It is not always the child's fault. An administrator's job is to recognized the type of luggage students bring with them and how much of the environment is causing the luggage to open on the wrong end.

N.F.eL

Technology should not be used only as a means to do work.
It should be used or thought of as an opportunity to
increase one's cognitive ability and to provide the
opportunity for increased introspection of one's work
or applied theory at work.

I don't think there is a teacher out there who doesn't complain about students not taking the initiative to develop and create new ideas with the knowledge they have taught. In this chapter you will see that students are creative when they want to be.

Although the school police officer may be new to the building as well as to the job, one of his greatest strengths has been to build a trusting relationship with some of the students. This relationship has provided us with valuable support and valuable information. As they say, information is power.

It was 7:00 A.M. on a cold January morning. I don't even think the sun had come up yet. The news reports said that we would be lucky if the temperature rose to five degrees today. I haven't felt this kind of cold since my college days at the University of Vermont. The cold gnawed like fire and could kill an exposed human being in minutes.

Francisco reported to Officer Mercer that two students got on the school bus yesterday and began to beat on him. He also claimed that the students jumped out of the emergency exit while the bus was in motion.

I looked at Officer Mercer and said, "That's why Junior and Hector jumped off the back of the bus yesterday afternoon. And it looks like Hector is up to this threatening stuff again."

We got a report that two of our students jumped off the bus while it was going down the street yesterday afternoon. We caught one student, but the other one ran away after we called out his name. We never got a chance to contact the bus driver to see what had happened. This story was starting to get much bigger than first suspected.

"Francisco, why did they want to beat you up?" I asked.

He said, "Last week, I told them that I didn't want to be part of the gang any more."

"Gang? What gang is that?"

"The N. F. eL.," he responded.

"Which stands for what?"

With a hesitating voice he said, "Um, Niggaz For Eternal Life. I got the book at home; you can have it all. It will tell you who all of them are."

Officer Mercer answered with his old-fashioned southern drawl, "Bring it in. Bring it in tomorrow, okay?"

Francisco slowly nodded yes.

I thought to myself, *These kids are something else. Francisco sits up in here, in his JROTC uniform. He's admitting he is not showing respect to the U.S. army uniform, and we know his family has been trying to raise more than a gangbanger.*

Officer Mercer said, "You know, Mr. Allen, when you get a hold of that book you are going to have to do a lot of running."

"Me? What did I do?" Officer Mercer has an insidious grin on his face; the kind of grin that deserves to be slapped off.

"You know how those gangs are. They are going to get Francesco for being a snitch and they are going to get you for knowing too much."

"Trust me; when I read it, you'll be sitting right next to me getting the dirt. Mercer knows everything, I'll proclaim. He forced that boy into giving the goods to the cops," I quipped back.

"That's cold, Mr. Allen."

"Hey," I shrugged.

The next day Francisco secretly handed the purple, crinkled notebook to Officer Mercer, who brought it to me. "Here you go, Mr. Allen."

"What is that?"

"The bible."

At this point I was very disappointed. I expected a whole lot more then a beat-up notebook.

"Hey everybody, look at what Mercer got!" I shouted in the middle of the corridor. Officer Mercer's eyes began to water as he stomped his foot with laughter. The faculty and students strangely looked on as they walked by. Officer Mercer slowly pulled himself together.

"I owe you," Mercer mumbled.

"Is that what you two were talking about yesterday?" exclaimed one of the teachers still in the office.

We both nodded yes.

"Oh, I'm out of here," she said laughing her way out of the office.

Only the secretary Ms. P., Officer Mercer, and I were left in the office. "Okay, what do we have?"

I opened the book slowly. There was a momentary pause. "We got their colors and the affiliations. We have their signs and street code. So, a number one is a dope bitch. We have what they consider violation codes: (1) disrespecting a higher rank and (2) 'droping your flag.' The dummy didn't even spell dropping right. But hey, they put a lot of effort into this. Over eleven code violations, not including the six attachments."

"Excuse me, Mr. Allen." I stopped reading.

"Yes, Mr. Reyes?"

"I caught some of the boys passing this around during breakfast."

"What is it?"

"It has to do with the Internet. Supposedly they have started a website. I didn't think it was appropriate for them to be passing this around in school so I took it from them."

"WWW.Niggaz4et.Life. You have to be sh—"

"Mr. Allen!" interjected Ms. P.

"Yes, Ms. P.," I said sheepishly.

"Just a reminder." said Ms. P. in a high-pitched voice that re-minded me of Sally, Charlie Brown's baby sister.

"I can't get these knuckleheads to do schoolwork, but they have time to pass this junk out. This is a joke, right?" I decided to leave the outer office and proceed to my inner sanctuary, where I have my own computer and the privacy sometimes needed to complete my job. I typed in the derogatory title and pressed enter. Up pops, "Warning!!! For Real Niggaz Only!!!"

Underneath the title was a picture of a police officer holding a donut. Then the following appears:

Don't Be A Dick!!! You have now entered the home of the N.F.eL. To put it is simple terms, N.F.eL. Is the newest, hottest, and ex-citing group in Beantown A.K.A. Boston. Most people know of other groups as Crips, Folk, and BK . . . We are a mixture of a rap group/hustlers/ballers/and pretty boyz in 1 tight package.

"Mercer, come here please!" I said in a loud but concerned tone.

Mercer inquired, "You found something?"

I turned the computer monitor around for Officer Mercer to see.

"These are your kids, Mr. Allen," he laughed.

"My kids?"

"Yeah, you told all those parents at the beginning of the year that you were going to adopt these kids and call them your own, while they were here at the Annex. So, what you gonna do now, *Dad?*"

I glared at Mercer out of the corner of my eyes. Who does he think he is, using my own words against me? I'll get him back later. I continued on as if he didn't say a word at all. As I spoke, I contin-ued to surf the web to take my mind off his comment and to act like his joke didn't faze me. "I want you to call the gang unit and get them in here. And I don't want the lieutenant here. They can send anyone they want, but not him."

"Are you going to call the students' parents?" Mercer wanted to know.

"No, I'm going to let them hang themselves. Right now, we have the upper hand, and I want to keep it that way. The next time they yell out 'four,' we know they are going to fight. 'Three' they are going to rob someone and so on. Let them do the work for us," I suggested.

Later I asked Officer Mercer, "Three weeks ago I asked you to call the gang unit."

"I did."

"They never showed up."

"I called several times and they said we were a low priority."

"Low priority? Ms P., don't you have connections in the mayor's office?"

"Yes, do you want me to make a call?"

"I think it's time. Officer Mercer, didn't you tell me earlier that the lieutenant got a promotion?"

"That's what I heard."

"What are the chances that he is behind the slow response?"

"He won't be for long after I make this phone call," chuckled Ms. P.

"I'll be at a training next week with the lieutenant. I'll ask him what is going on," said Officer Mercer.

The next day, two police units showed up at the Annex. They were given copies of the "bible" and all of the students' names and addresses. One of the officers said as he pointed at one of the drawings, "We've been looking for the person that has been doing this tag. This has been all over the Ruggles Orange line T station. I wish we had gotten this weeks ago."

A week later I asked Mercer, "Well, what did the lieutenant say?"

"I asked him why he didn't send anyone over to the Annex when we called. He asked me if you were still here. I told him yes. He then said he got the information and checked it out and he thought that it wasn't important. I told him that if something happens here it is on his head, not ours."

"That's it?"

"He just turned his back to me and walked away."

"Well, Mr. Allen, it looks to me that you were right about the lieutenant being behind the lack of response from the police," said Ms. P.

"Thanks for making the call. I should have gone with my instincts last year and followed through on bringing formal charges on him. Shame on me once."

Some of us think of our students and the relationships they build as unimportant child's play, their deepest thoughts as inconsequential. Apparently some of our students are very serious about their activities. Even though they pay no taxes, still they place high value—ownership, even—on the turf they defend with their lives. Even though we know that after high school, the likelihood of the longevity of our students' attachments and relationships is nil, still, some consider themselves "Niggaz For Eternal Life." To correct some of our issues in education we've got to stay five steps ahead and meet our students halfway.

3/14/00 INCIDENT: BOMB THREAT
TO ANNEX IN HYDE PARK

"**M**ass. State Police recording an emergency."

"Hello! Hello!"

"Hello!" the state police officer said loudly in a slightly agitated tone.

"There is a bomb in . . . in our school. My friend told me about it this morning."

"Yeah, where is the bomb?"

"It's in . . . he . . . he told me it is in the basement."

"The basement of what school?" The state police officer asked.

"H-Hyde Park. Please come and help." Then the voice was cut off.

"HHH."

"Hyde Park Annex. Please come and help us. Tell them to send someone fast—Hyde Park Annex." The student caller hung up the phone.

The state police officer then called the Boston police.

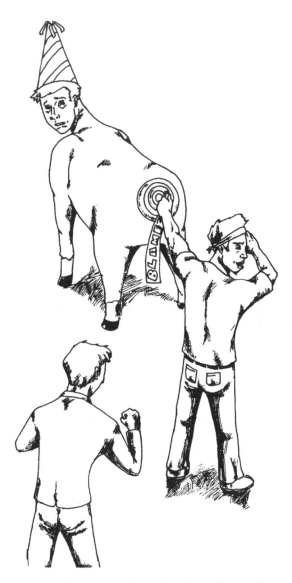

Blame: Another name for pin the tail on the donkey.

"Boston Police, this line is recording. Do you have an emergency?" said the female in a dry and unassuming voice.

"Hi. Boston State here. Just got a cell phone call from a kid saying he's in the Hyde Park Annex and there's a bomb in the basement."

"Say anything else?"

"No, that's all. He said, 'Hurry send someone quick there's a bomb in the basement at the Hyde Park Annex.'"

"Telephone number or anything?"

"Ah, no. Nothing."

"Okay. Your name, sir?" The state officer gave his name and then spelled it for the female Boston officer.

"Your number?" asked the Boston police officer. The state police officer gave his number to the Boston police officer.

"Thank you very much, sir."

"Mr. Allen, the Boston police are out front looking for you," said Ms. P.

"Me?" I asked with one eyebrow meeting my receding hairline. (As much frowning as I do, I'm surprised I don't have more wrinkles on my forehead.) "What do they want with me?"

"I don't know, Mr. Allen." Ms. P. moved close to my ear and whispered, "The one I saw had a bomb squad jacket on."

"Go around to all of the classes and tell the teachers to remain in their rooms with their students," I instructed. "You and I will have to communicate with each other in person, in other words, no radios."

I had gone through one of these bomb threats two months ago. The whole school had to be emptied out in ten-below weather. The students had to remain outside for ninety minutes before they could go back in after the building was determined to be all clear. They had no jackets and the surrounding businesses wouldn't let them in to warm up. March in New England isn't much warmer than December. If my Annex children have to freeze their little buns again to get the message that I will not send them home for a false alarm, then so be it.

I went out and approached the police officer. "Yes, officer, how can I help you?"

"Are you in charge?" he asked.

"Yes, I am. How can I help you?" I said.

"We have a call that a bomb threat was made to this school," he said matter-of-factly.

"I didn't receive any calls here and I didn't make one to you."

"The call went into the state police," he pointed out to me.

"You're not state police," I said in a "so what are you doing here?" sort of way.

"The state police called us."

I asked, "Are you going to check the building?"

"Well, you know the building better than I so why don't you and your people check the building."

"Excuse me?" I said. I hate when they pull this crap. They don't want to do their job because they know it is a false alarm. "You're the bomb expert."

"It's probably nothing. It was a generic threat."

"A generic threat?" I asked, as I raised my eyebrow.

"Yeah, like 'I'm going to fuckin' blow up your school.' You never need to worry unless they start to tell you what time and where it is. That kind of specific information."

"You aren't going to search, are you?" I wanted to cut to the chase.

"No, you can."

I looked him dead in his eyes and tilted my chin down and said, "They got names for people like you." The names I was thinking of were not very nice.

The Boston police officer laughed, unaffected by what I had said, and I headed off to search my building. I didn't let the students out of the school this time. If I had, it would have created a feeding frenzy on bomb threats to the school. When I was done, I returned to the police officer.

"I didn't find anything suspicious. Do you have the number they called from?" I asked.

"No. The state police don't have 911 enhanced."

"Can I get a recording of the call that was made?" I wanted to see if I recognized the voice of the person making the call.

"Hmm, I don't know. I've never been asked that before. I'll get back to you."

"Cool . . . Mercer!!"

"Mr. Allen."

"It's time to go hunting."

"Big fish or little fish."

"I want the whole school."

A couple of days later I received the tape recording.

I said, "Mercer, come here. I want you to listen to this."

"Oh, you 'gots' your tape." I pressed play. "Hey, I know who that is. That's that kid they call Trinnie. Don't he know you can't hide that accent?" Mercer said.

"Bring him in here."

A few minutes later, Trinnie arrived. "Yes, Mr. Allen?"

"I want you to listen to something." I began to play the tape for Trinnie. "Does that voice sound familiar to you?"

Trinnie answered with a definitive no.

I must admit I didn't expect him to say yes. Like a throwback to the days when I mixed music tapes, I began to repeat a section of the tape to him. "There is a bomb in . . . in our school. There is a bomb . . . a bomb in . . . in our. A bomb a bomb."

"Sound familiar yet?" I asked.

Again, Trinnie responded with a no. But his eyes said, *I'm fucked.*

"I want you to come in tomorrow morning with your parents to see if they can recognize any of the voices on this tape," I said.

The next morning both of his parents came in. They were a mixed couple. The man he called Dad was his stepfather. He was a short, stocky white man who fell in love with a Jamaican woman on a visit to the island. "Good morning. I'm glad to see you both. I have a tape I would like you to hear."

"Don't bother, Mr. Allen. It was him. He told us about it last night. We came in to make him tell you the whole story," said his stepdad.

"Man . . . you all took my fun away. I have a special way of playing the tape for you," I kidded.

"Yeah, he told us about that too. You got him good." The young man's father turned to him, nudged him, and said, "Tell him the whole thing," he warned.

"I can't," Trinnie replied.

The stepdad asked, "Go on, or do you want to go back to Jamaica?"

"Okay, okay. Mr. Allen, I didn't mean to cause you any problem."

"What do you call making a bomb threat? Those kinds of practical jokes can lead to five years in prison or a $10,000 fine. Do you have $10,000?"

Trinnie explained, "No. They told me it would just get us out of school early."

"Who are they?" I wanted to know.

"I can't say," Trinnie replied.

The father interrupted again, "I know there are no guarantees, but if you don't want Mr. Allen to call the police or expel you from school, I think you need to tell him everything."

"Your dad is right. Under 7.10.5 of the code of discipline it states making a bomb threat may result in suspension to expulsion. The recommendation will be mine. This is totally on you," I said.

Trinnie continued, "It was Chris, John, and Harold."

"How were they involved?" I inquired.

"Harold thought of the idea. He then asked Chris and John to write down what I should say." Trinnie pulled a crumbled piece of paper out of his pocket and handed it to me.

"Is this what they wrote?" I asked.

Reluctantly, Trinnie replied, "Yes."

"Let me see your notebook," I asked. Trinnie reached into his backpack and pulled out his spiral-bound book and handed it to me. I compared the writing, and none of it matched his writing. "Okay, it doesn't match. Go on."

Trinnie went on, "After they handed me the note, Harold gave me his cell phone. I went into the bathroom and made the call."

"Then what?" I asked.

"I went back to class. They asked me did I do it? I told them yes."

"Is there anything else?"

"No." He appear both honest and resolute.

"I will continue my investigation. Trinnie, you're suspended for five days. I will contact you and your parents within three days to let you know if there will be an expulsion hearing."

"Okay, Mr. Allen. Thank you for this chance. Please, please don't expel me. I didn't mean to hurt you. And I don't want to hurt my parents," Trinnie pleaded.

I said to myself, *I can't let him off that easy. I need to give him something to think about.* I looked Trinnie in the eyes and said, "Son, let's just hope your story pans out."

I walked all three of them to the front door. On my walk back to my office I devised my plan to get the other three boys.

"Ms. P., page the English teachers of Chris and John and tell them to send writing samples of those boys to me," I requested.

When the samples arrived, I compared them to the note. Chris appeared to have written 75 percent of the note. I then called each boy to my office individually. I told each one that the others "dimed" him out. In the end, they ended up telling the same story that Trinnie told. Both students were given their suspension hearing letters and were sent home after their parents were called.

"Ms. P., please page Harold to my office."

Harold came in and sat down. "What?" he demanded to know.

I didn't answer. I just leaned over and handed him his suspension and expulsion papers.

"What is this? You can't do this for nothing," Harold protested.

"It's all on the paper. Take it home to your mother and return on the date of the hearing."

"I didn't do anything," he insisted.

"The other three said you did."

"No they didn't," he said, angrily.

"Yes, they did. Go home." I was curt to punctuate the point.

After Harold left, I sent his mother a certified letter of the hearing and left her a message on the phone. I decided to expel him because of his compounded violations of the code of discipline.

Harold arrived with his mother, Ms. Verona, seven days later—four days late.

"Hello, Ms. Verona. Thank you for coming in. I need to let you know that because this is an expulsion hearing, this meeting will be recorded. Also, there is a script in the code of discipline I must follow. So I will be doing a lot of reading in this hearing." I proceeded to press record and read the script. "Good morning. My name is Mr. Allen. I am assistant headmaster in charge of the Annex. I shall be serving as the hearing officer for this matter. The date is March 24, 2000. The time is 8:00 A.M. The hearing is being conducted at the Annex."

"The purpose of the hearing is to consider the possible expulsion of Harold Verona for alleged violations of the code of discipline sections 7.10.5 making a bomb threat, 7.2.3 assault and battery on any person, and 7.11.1 repeated and flagrant violations of the code. Will those present please identify themselves for the record?"

Harold stated his name. His mother did the same.

I continued to read the script. "As the hearing officer, I must warn you that the records of this hearing may be subpoenaed in court. Therefore, if you, Harold, wish to remain silent you may do so, and the fact that you remain silent will not in any way be interpreted as an admission of guilt. Ms. Verona, did you receive notification of this hearing to consider expulsion?"

"No, I did *not*."

"Please let the record show that Ms. Verona has answered with a no." I continued, "On March 17, a certified letter was sent to the address listed with the school and signed for by what looks like Ms. Verona's signature."

"Oh yeah, I did get that," she said with embarrassment as she realized that she was caught.

"Did you receive notification of your right to representation?"

"Yes."

"Let the record show that the parent, Ms. Verona, has answered affirmatively." Later when Harold was asked to tell his side of the story, his mother refused to let him speak. She said she wanted to go "on record."

Ms. Verona protested on the record, "I want it to be known that you have been out to get my son all year. You've been blaming him for this gang stuff, fighting, and now this bomb stuff. He is in this situation because of you."

"Miss, hold on. I am not the one who told or encouraged your son to design a website claiming he's a 'baller and hustler.' I never suggested he should pass out flyers in school to recruit members to his gang. I didn't tell him to try to strangle a girl on the way home from school. Nor did I ever tell him to come back during his suspension and trespass at the school upstairs. And by the way, you may have forgotten, while he was up there, he attacked a boy he got into an argument with. I didn't tell your son to come up with a plan to threaten to blow up a school, and I surely didn't tell him to use his personal cell phone. Your son did this to himself. Harold was provided with every opportunity to straighten himself out. So don't blame me."

"I am blaming you!" She insisted.

To myself, *That's right, blame the black man.*

I hate expelling students, but sometimes it is a necessary evil. As an administrator, I certainly have to deal with all threats to the public safety. John Dewey (1938) writes in his book *Experience and Education*:

> I am not romantic enough about the young to suppose that every pupil will respond or that any child of normally strong impulses

will respond on every occasion. There are likely to be some who, when they come to school, are already victims of injurious conditions outside of the school and who have become so passive and unduly docile that they fail to contribute. There will be others who, because of previous experience, are bumptious and unruly and perhaps downright rebellious. But it is certain that the general principle of social control cannot be predicated upon such cases. It is also true that no general rule can be laid down for dealing with such cases. The teacher has to deal with them individually. They fall into general classes, but no two are exactly alike. The educator has to discover as best he or she can the causes for the recalcitrant attitudes. He or she cannot, if the educational process is to go on, make it a question of pitting one will against another in order to see which is stronger, nor yet allow the unruly and non-participating pupils to stand permanently in the way of the educative activities of others. Exclusion perhaps is the only available measure at a given juncture, but it is no solution. For it may strengthen the very causes which have brought about the undesirable anti-social attitude. (56)

Furthermore, the current policy of looking at data to improve education (the standards movement) forces schools to overlook the social isolation factors that urban students face, leaving them vulnerable to an increase in disruptive behavior, potentially increasing the number of exclusions from school. Don't get me wrong! Data is useful. I use it to help define what students are weak in so that task-specific curricula can be designed to fit the needs of the students. But those who collect data don't care about and can't (or won't) factor in joblessness or homelessness and the many other problems that manifest themselves in our schools. These are outside variables that are considered excuses for not getting the job done. As Bob Chase comments in *Will Standards Save Public Education?*:

If the standards movement does not provide ample means for all students to meet higher academic expectations, it will prove to be one of the cruelest hoaxes in American history, right up there with Horatio Alger. (Meier et al. 2000, 42)

I'VE GOT THE POWER: SHAWN

*Those who are perceived to have simple minds
can create the most complex issues.*

Bang! Bam!

"What was that?"

As I turned around, I saw a teacher run out of her classroom and head into the room next door. As I quickly walked back in that direction, the teacher exited the room. I watched her face intently, as her terrified frown turned into a smile. "It's Shawn again," she said. Shawn is an autistic boy who loves to draw. In fact, his work is so inspiring it belongs in a museum. But his autism makes him hard to deal with if you are not prepared for his impromptu antics. Specifically, Shawn has been diagnosed with Asperger's syndrome. Tony Attwood (1998) states that a child diagnosed with Asperger's syndrome lacks social skills and empathy, has a limited ability to have a reciprocal conversation, and has an intense interest in a particular subject (e.g., art, music, trains).

The teacher continued, "He said he is angry because Ms. Marshall came into the room and didn't say hi to him." Ms. Marshall is a chunky woman who loves to wear overly tight clothes. Her garments show every roll and accentuate her top-heavy body.

Ms. Marshall, who was standing by the classroom at this point said, "God, I was only in there for a second. He can't be throwing these temper tantrums to get my attention."

The teacher waddled into the classroom, stood over Shawn, and said hello. She immediately turned around and ran out. She closed the door behind her and rested her forehead on the door. Shaking her head, she said, "Omigod! Do you know what he is doing?"

"No," I said in the driest voice I could produce.

"When I looked down, he showed me his thing," she said pointing to her groin. "He has his pants down and he has his blue down jacket covering himself. I said, 'Hi Shawn' and he just flopped it down to expose himself."

With a big grin, "Well, Ms. Marshall, can you tell me what you've been doing to encourage this student?"

"That's not funny, Mr. Allen. Someone needs to do something," Ms. Marshall said.

"Don't you understand? He wants to show you how much he likes you." I don't think she got the hint that the way she dresses might have had something to do with the extra attention Shawn wanted to give her.

"Ok, Mr. Allen. Are you going to do something?"

Laughing. "I'll take care of it." I took a second to calm myself. I figured I was going to have fun with this episode. I can't get upset at him. This antisocial behavior is indicative of Asperger's syndrome. I spent too much time disciplining kids who have no excuse for their behavior. This was a special situation and I was going to treat it as such. I strutted into the classroom, using my best imitation of Eddy Murphy imitating Clint Eastwood. "Shawn, I hear you've been doing some . . . inappropriate things."

Shawn, sounding like McGruff on steroids said, "How did you know?"

How did I know? repeating Shawn's words to myself. I paused and stared hard into Shawn's eyes. My eyes were ready to pop out of my cranium. I spoke slowly and deliberately like Eastwood, right before he pulls the trigger in *Dirty Harry*. "I have ESP," I said.

Shawn stared up at me with his brown eyes also wide open. He slowly brought his fingertips to the bend at his bottom lip and said, "How did you get such power?"

"I've always had . . . the *power*. And it's telling me you're doing nasty things. Now pull your pants up and get outside," I demanded.

Shawn started squirming in his seat and shifted his weight from left to right as he shimmed his carpenter pants up his backside. He immediately followed me outside of the classroom. When we got outside, Shawn watched my every move.

I continued, "I know you know how to be appropriate." Shawn nodded yes. "I know you do. And I know when you're choosing to be bad."

"But how did you get such power?" Shawn insisted.

"I told you, I've always had it. And I'm going to watch your every move and your every thought (pointing at his head). When I receive your thought that you're going to misbehave, I'll be right behind you. Now, when you go back into the classroom, I don't want any banging on the desk, yelling, or any other kind of inappropriate behavior. Do you understand?" I said forcefully.

"Yes." Shawn slowly started to walk into the classroom. I could see him staring at the doorframe from the corner of his eyes. He tried so hard to be slick.

"Don't kick . . . the door."

"How did you know?" Shawn asked.

"I told you. Now this is your last chance." Shawn stiffened his body as rigidly as a toy soldier as he walked into the room. His steps were slow and deliberate. The concentration he took was amazing to watch as he battled with himself to stay well behaved.

An hour later I went back to visit Shawn. " Shawn." He turned around and stared. "That plan you're working on isn't going to work," I said convincingly.

Shawn snapped, "How did you know?"

"Mr. Allen."

"Yes," I responded to the new custodian who was coming out of the boys' bathroom as I was walking back to my office after lunch duty. You could see the disgust on his face.

"I heard you know how to handle that boy Shawn."

"Well, you don't really handle Shawn. You just have to stay one step ahead of him."

"No really. Someone gots to do something about that boy."

"What did he do now?"

"I'm getting tired of cleaning up after the boy," the custodian complained.

"Well, isn't that your job?" I responded with a puzzled and slightly annoyed voice.

"Part of my job is to clean the bathroom after an emergency or at the end of the day when the kids are all gone. It is not to clean up after him every time they let him go to the bathroom."

"What's he doing, peeing on the floor?"

"No. They leave him in there too long to be by himself. Then they call me to clean up his mess."

"I'm sorry. I don't get it." I was truly perplexed.

"They let him stand in front of the wall and whack off and squirt up the whole thing. Then they call me to clean up his mess."

I paused for a moment imagining myself cleaning up that type of mess from someone else. I stared at the custodian. I grinned and shook my head in disbelief and said, "Sorry, I can't help you."

The custodian said, "That's wrong. I thought you were cool," he laughed.

Still grinning I said, "Seriously, I will talk to his teachers and ask them to send a male para to the bathroom with Shawn. The male para should be able to go into the bathroom after Shawn to break up *his routine.*"

"I hope that works," said the custodian, "'cause it is real nasty when he gets done in there."

Shawn displays many of the criteria for Asperger's syndrome in terms of social behavior, language, interest and routine, motor clumsiness, cognition and sensory sensitivity. Atwood writes, "Sula Wolff (1995) has recently written . . . They tend to be solitary and emotionally detached, yet sensitive to criticism. They do not conform to conventional social rules and have unusual metaphorical speech" (184).

In Shawn's case it was important to recognize what was the cause of the inappropriate behavior and to develop a plan of action to end the unwanted act and replace it with a constructive one. Part of the step-by-step plan would include clues the student would recognize signaling to him that he would need to find other means of stimulating himself while he is in school.

So much of an administrator's job is "smoke and mirrors," although students may believe we have the power. The reality is that the power has always belonged to them. They simply surrender it to us occasionally. Nonetheless, it is critical we maintain the illusion—if we are going to survive.

NOT SUCH A GOOD BOY AFTER ALL

*It will be a legitimate expression of conscience when
schools can teach a series of social development skills that
encourage students to make good decisions and which
inform them of the consequences of their decisions
without the fear of being blamed.*

"**M**r. Allen, did you read the paper today?" Mercer had that grin again, meaning you have no choice but to get sucked in. He has information you need to know, and it is information that I'm going to have to deal with or at least to explore.

"No, I didn't. What is it about?"

Mercer continues, "The kids told me that the car crash with the two old ladies was caused by Hector."

"Get the blip out."

"No, seriously. If you've noticed, he isn't here and his girlfriend isn't either. Here is the article. Read it." Mercer handed me the newspaper.

A high-speed chase through Mattapan ended early yesterday when a 15-year-old driving at least 80 mph slammed into a moving car and sent two women to the hospital, police said . . . The juvenile fled the scene and didn't stop until he again lost control of his car and crashed into a grate in front of the Sunny Cigar Store on Cummings Highway (Richardson 2000).

"Hector isn't such a good boy after all. Serves his mommy right. I warned that woman. She didn't want to listen. She just wanted to 'blame the black man.' The same black man she'll be calling for help this afternoon. But I'm going to beat her to the punch. I'm going to give her a call, asking if she would like some assistance with her *good* boy. Where's my phone?" I said.

"Right here, Mr. Allen," said Ms. P.

"Thanks. Do you have that number?"

"I'll get it if you want it."

"Thanks. You're too good for me, Ms. P."

"I know. So don't you forget it," She said with a smile.

"Hello. This is Mr. Allen from the Annex calling. How are you doing, Ms. Rodriguez? I heard some disturbing news about Hector."

"Yes, yes, I don't know what he was thinking," she complained

"Well, the school just wants to know if he is okay."

"He is a little bruised but he is fine. He is in lockup right now. We just don't know how to get him out. Do you think if we promise to send him to Florida, they would let him go?"

"Well Miss, I don't know about that. He caused a lot of damage and he hurt a couple of elderly people."

"There must be something that you can do to help Hector, Mr. Allen," she said, forcing the words from her mouth.

"All I can suggest is that you present this idea to your attorney. Maybe he can manipulate it in Hector's favor," I suggested with genuine concern.

"Okay, I will try that. Thank you, Mr. Allen, for your concern."

"Good-bye and good luck, Miss. Send me a letter letting me know when I can sign him out of school," I added.

"Okay."

"All right then. Bye."

I learned over time not to feel guilty when I have done all I can for a student. I've tried many types of disciplinary action over the years. Community service was a wonderful idea and much more effective than suspension but obviously much harder to manage. It even became more difficult as we became more effective at disseminating the consequences. The school became so clean it was hard to find things for the students to do. Our students didn't just sweep the classroom floors or wash whiteboards, they scraped gum from underneath the desks, washed graffiti from walls, desks, and chairs, and performed other creative duties my teachers devised.

I always got permission from the parents before the community service was given out. I presented the idea to the parents as an alternative to having their child suspended from school. The parents usually agreed to the idea of having their child stay after school to do work instead of missing school. You know it is an effective measure when a child begs his guardian to please just let him be suspended.

I've had one parent complain about the service. The student brought an "aunt" to the hearing. During the hearing the aunt and the student agreed to punishment, which was dealt at the end of the day. The young man was given an assignment to scrape used gum from underneath the desks. A few weeks later the mother came in complaining about what I made her child do. I told her that her son's aunt came in and signed the agreement. The parent responded by saying that her son didn't have an aunt. I showed her the note I kept on file giving me permission to talk to the aunt. The woman responded by saying it wasn't her signature. It turned out the young man convinced a stranger off the street to be his guardian for the day. Unfortunately it was impossible for me to verify who this person was at the time because the mother's home information as well as her telephone number were listed wrong. I now refuse to talk to anyone not listed as the guardian. And if for some strange extreme reason I break my own rule to verify the substitute guardian in front of me via the phone, I take a copy of his or her driver's license and keep it on file.

THAT'S JUST AN S
ACROSS MY FOREHEAD

Principals who administrate solely by their hearts,
get schooled.

"**M**r. Allen, can I talk to you?"

"Sure Toya, come on in." Toya is a medium-size, light cocoa brown–skinned girl. She has a fair number of friends and for the most part stays out of trouble. "Well, what do you need to talk about?"

"My mother assaulted me last night."

"That is a very serious charge, Toya. What makes you believe that?" I asked.

"Mr. Allen, I told her I was pregnant and she just started screaming and going wild."

"I think I would have gone nuts if my fourteen-year-old daughter told me she was pregnant."

"Mr. Allen, she attacked me. She shoved me against the wall, then she took my book bag and hit me with it. I'm all bruised up," Toya said, seeking some sympathy.

I started to feel the pain she was expressing to me. I could see little tears forming in her eyes as she gestured about each blow she had received. I called for the school nurse to check out the extent of

Toya's injuries. I wanted to be clear to DSS about all the details of the incident. After returning with the nurse from her office, the nurse confirmed several marks on the girl's neck and back. Before sending Toya back to her classroom, I told her of my plan to call DSS. When my office was finally empty and the door completely closed, I made my call to the agency.

"Hey guys, this is Mr. Allen at the Annex. I have a fourteen-year-old girl here claiming her mother attacked her when she found out the daughter was pregnant."

The person at the agency asked, "How does the girl appear?"

"The nurse checked her out and found bruises on her neck and back."

The woman at DSS then asked to speak to Toya, who was brought to my office to speak to the DSS worker. When she was done, she handed the phone back to me so I could finish my interview with the DSS caseworker. The questions continued like this until the last one. The woman at the agency asked me if I had spoken to the parent yet. I told her no. Our procedure was to call DSS first. The woman asked me to call the parent and then get back to her.

"You want me to call her? I thought you guys were the ones who were supposed to do the investigating?" I asked. I thought to myself, *DSS does not identify the reporter. They expect you to do it yourself. This process is supposed to be confidential.*

"I find it easier on the parents when the school calls about the claims being made," she said.

I felt agitated at this point. "Fine, I will make the call." I didn't want to call the mother. People say I make it look like it is nothing, but I hate dealing with parents in tough situations. They are worse than the kids.

"Hello, may I speak to the parent or guardian of Toya Clancy."

"This is she speaking," Toya's mother said.

"This is Mr. Allen calling from the Annex. Toya came to me with a serious complaint today."

Ms. Clancy sighed.

"She said that you hit her with her book bag, causing the bruises on her neck and back."

"What would I want to do that for?" said Ms. Clancy in a very sarcastic way, emphasizing the "what" and "would" and drawing out the "for."

I'm missing something, I thought. The facts of this case weren't adding up. "She said you did it because she told you she was pregnant."

"No! No! My baby no! Oh my God! Oh my God! No, Mr. Allen. No. I thought my baby was a virgin. I didn't know she was having sex," she said, as she began to cry over the phone.

"Miss, are you going to be okay?" At this point I was really fishing for answers.

The woman sniffled and said, "Yes, Mr. Allen. I swear I didn't beat that child. I yelled at her for coming home late and that was it. She never said anything about thinking she was pregnant. Where is my baby now? I need to hug her. I need to talk to her."

"I sent her back to class. After I complete my investigation, either myself or she will give you a call."

"Is there a problem with her calling her mother?"

"Any time a student makes a report about abuse the school is obligated to investigate the claim and report it to DSS."

"Do I have to have them in my family's business?" she wanted to know.

"If Toya backs your story, then they will go away. By the way, where did Toya get the bruises and scratches from?" I asked.

"She was with her father last weekend and she fell off her bike. I know it is hard to believe but she did. You just ask her."

"Okay, I will." We said our good-byes and I asked Ms. P. to page Toya back to my office.

"Yes, Mr. Allen."

"Sit down. I just spoke to your mother. She didn't know *what* I was talking about. In fact, when I told her the part about you being pregnant, she screamed, 'No, my baby no.' So tell me again what happened." Toya was looking down as she watched herself pick at the cuticle of her index finger.

"I came home and my mother started yelling at me because I was late."

"And?"

"That's it."

"And where did the bruises come from?"

"I fell off my bike last weekend."

"So what about this 'she beat me with a book bag' stuff?"

"I was scared to tell her that I was pregnant."

"You *used* me. Call your mother!"

Is that just an *S* across my forehead? Or do people use the power they perceive in my position to their advantage? As a public servant, am I obligated to respond in kind to the emotional tempests lurking beneath the surface of my everyday encounters?

SURROGATE DAD

*When mothers call you for guidance on
their child's home issues, you have reached the top.*

8:10 P.M. The phone rang in my small one-bedroom apartment.

"Hello."

"Hello, Mr. Allen. This is the sergeant from the BPS police office. I received a report of a missing boy by the name of James Feldon."

"I'm sorry, but I don't know who that is."

The sergeant answered, "Well, he is the six-year-old brother of Shanis Washington."

"Sergeant, I know this is important, but what does it have to do with me?"

"I'm wondering if you know who Shanis's friends are?"

"Sergeant, do you know where Shanis is?" I asked

"Yes," said the sergeant.

"Then why don't you ask her?" It seemed like the most logical thing to do.

"Let me start over again, Mr. Allen. Shanis was supposed to pick up her little brother after school, but she didn't. She asked one of her friends to do it and she can't remember his name."

"What? Get out of here. That girl hangs out with so many people, I wouldn't know where to begin." I gave the sergeant a list of names off the top of my head, and I wished him good luck. Before we hung up, I asked him to call me when they located the little boy. At 10:30 P.M. I was notified that the boy had been found unharmed.

The next day at 7:00 A.M., Ms. Washington, Shanis, and James came to my office.

"Mr. Allen," said Ms. Washington, "I need to tell you what happened so you can talk to this girl." I understand that we administrators play a lot of different roles, but this woman is acting like this is my kid. "This girl leaves her little brother with . . . with . . . What is his name?

"Paul," Shanis said with her hands clenched together and her face toward the floor.

"She forgot the boy's name. She didn't know his phone number. She doesn't even know were he lives. The boy was walking around the city with my son. When we found them, finally, it was because the boy's mother contacted the police about a lost little boy her son brought home."

I looked at James; he grabbed his mom by the waist and gave me a quick smile. "He looks like he's doing okay," I said.

"I took him to the doctor last night to get checked out. The doctor said he is fine," continued the mother.

"Shanis, what were you thinking? You could have permanently lost your little brother," I said.

"It's not like that, Mr. Allen. You know Paul. He is a good kid," cried Shanis.

"I know Paul in school, not out of school. I don't know if he is a responsible person. Do you know if he likes little boys?" Shanis paused and looked at her mother.

"You know what he means; answer him," her mother snapped.

"No," Shanis said in an embarrassed voice.

I continued, "Paul is about five feet eleven inches and weighs about two hundred pounds. James, come here please. I'm going to hold onto your coat and I want you to punch my arm and pull away from me as hard as you can."

James looked at his mother and she responded, "It's okay, honey, Mr. Allen won't hurt you. He just wants to show your sister something." Ms. Washington knew where I was coming from.

I took James by his left arm with my right and I rested my head on my desk, staring at Shanis. Then I told James to go. He tugged. He pulled. He hit and groaned in frustration that he couldn't get away. "Paul outweighs me by sixty pounds. Just in the way that I controlled this situation, any grown man could control your little brother and have their way with him. If you have the big sister responsibility to pick him up after school, then you need to follow through on your obligations."

"I just wanted a little time for myself," cried Shanis.

"That's a discussion between you and your mom. You should have that discussion before you take matters into your own hands. Miss, have a talk with Shanis when she gets home. Now I have to move on and start the school day."

"Mr. Allen, thank you," she said, beaming and genuinely grateful.

"You're welcome, Miss. James, it was nice meeting you." I walked the mother and James to the front door and sent Shanis to her homeroom. There is always that moment when I get to take a deep breath. I look forward to the precious time before the next crisis arrives. Sometimes the crisis is five seconds away; sometimes half a day, or even happening while I'm trying to resolve the present one. But I'm always aware that it is just around the corner and this little break is the only time I get to prepare myself.

It was about ten o'clock when the next unscheduled parent arrived. "Ms. Johnson, what can I do for you?" I asked.

"I need you to bring John in here and search him."

"What for, Miss?"

"I left $200 on the kitchen table to pay the rent and it was gone this morning," the mother protested.

"Ms. Johnson, this is a home problem, not a problem for the school," I warned.

"Mr. Allen, I need my rent money and I know that boy has it. I will write it down that you have my permission to search him," she insisted.

"Ms. Johnson, he is your son. You can search him anytime you want."

"And you're a man and he won't disrespect you like he disrespects me at home. Please help me, I need that money." It is always amazing to me, no matter how many times I encounter it, how easily some parents surrender their power to an authority they believe is higher than they are—when they hold the power all along.

"Okay, Ms. Johnson. I will get John, but I will warn you I won't be nice."

"That's fine, Mr. Allen," Ms. Johnson said, relieved.

I asked Ms. P. to page John to my office. John arrived two minutes later. He was smiling until he walked in and saw his mother sitting there waiting for him.

"John, where is my money?" She snapped immediately.

"What money?"

"The money I left on the table."

"I don't know what you did with it," he said while gesturing to his mom that she was crazy.

"It is the money for the rent. If I don't pay it, we don't have a place to live. So where is the money?"

"I don't know."

I walked up to John's face and said, "Empty out your pockets."

"What?" John said with a scowl on his face.

"You heard me. Empty out your pockets," I demanded.

"I don't have to do that if I don't want to."

"That's where you are wrong. As long as you are in my office with your mother giving me permission, I will and can search you." I took the risky chance and grabbed John by the arm and checked his inner coat pockets. On the second try, I pulled out a folded group of twenty-dollar bills. The money was handed over to Ms. Johnson, who began counting the stash. I continued, "Why would you do that to your own mother?"

"She knows. I told her."

"John, I told you yesterday that I didn't have the money this week, and if you wait two more weeks, I'd give you the money then."

"Excuse me, John, but what was so important that you had to steal from your own mother?" I asked.

John responded, "I told her I wanted some new Timberland boots. The ones with the blue fronts and the light gray leather."

I said, "John, I remember you showing me some new Timberland boots three weeks ago when you came to school. In fact, you have them on right now."

"Yeah? So? These aren't any good anymore; they have a scuff-mark on the toe. I can't walk around with this mark here."

I looked at Ms. Johnson and lifted one eyebrow and said, "Ms. Johnson, I'm sorry, but get your son out of my office."

Bill Cosby once said to Paula Zahn:

Talking. Talking. Parenting. Correctly parenting. That's what it's about. And you can't blame other things. You got to . . . you got to straighten up your house. Straighten up your apartment. Straighten up your child." He later continued, "What kept me out of trouble is going right to the edge and then . . . thinking that my mother would be embarrassed, and that I didn't want to embarrass her, and that my father would be embarrassed, and I just didn't want to do that to my family.

Without respect, or at a minimum fear, what is there to stop a child from misbehaving? It will be a legitimate expression of conscience when schools can teach a series of social development skills that encourage students to make good decisions and which inform them of the consequences of their decisions without the fear of being blamed.

Eventually I had to learn not to get overly involved in family matters. I can't fix every domestic problem that enters my office and

I surely can't fix issues that have been brewing for fifteen years. I can only dedicate my effort to do the best I can and support parents who are ready to make a positive move.

After this incident, the school year ended peacefully. Among the last things we had to do was pack up our substitute home, write our last report, and head back to the main building. During the last common planning meeting, I divided the Annex teachers into two groups and asked each group of teachers to answer two questions: Group 1 was asked, "Given the high-stakes elements in place for your incoming ninth grade classes, what are you doing or planning to engage students, their families, and the community as partners and allies in the high school restructuring process?" Group 2 was asked, "What lessons have you learned this year from piloting a key practice and planning for your implementation?"

The teachers in group 1 responded by stating:

As a faculty, our restructuring focuses on developing a thematic, interdisciplinary approach with our ninth grade students. Our curriculum explores teaching and learning through student-centered learning and experiential learning. Students are engaged in portfolio evaluations, critical thinking, cognitive development and problem solving.

The teachers in group 2 responded in part by stating:

We found the themes created increased cooperation and organization among teachers. The unity of themes also encouraged interdisciplinary teamwork among students and teachers. As a result, we found that the themes enhanced student academic performance and increased skill development; students began to make connections across disciplines with projects and field trips that connected the various classes themes and activities, and because teachers' curricula were coordinated, students had less of a chance to "slip through the cracks."

Annex teachers felt the portfolios held the students accountable for their work. The portfolios included each semester's culminating products. They stated, "The portfolios were a successful, student-centered method to focus students on taking responsibility for their work, to use the writing process, and developed their skills in producing and maintaining a long-term project. It also helped teachers focus the work toward a coordinated, whole-year effort."

Never once throughout this meeting did they complain about the kids. The teachers were more interested in figuring out ways to make the school more interesting for the students. They believed that if they could get more of the students actively engaged in school, they would be less likely to act out. They were proud of the work they had done. (Even now, in September 2005, students and teachers are still talking about the Annex and the positive effect it had on the school community.)

We headed back to the main building during its accreditation evaluation year. Although I had been away from the school for two years, the new headmaster placed me in charge of the process. This is a two-year process that I was only given four months to complete. When the final report came out, our Annex program received high commendations for the work that was done on thematic teaching and taking instruction beyond the school walls.

JUST SOMETHING TO DO AFTER SCHOOL

Generation Extreme: When did sex become an after school extracurricular activity?

"Mr. Allen, you've got to do something about those boys. They keep talking about me," said Tina.

"Are they telling you how pretty you are, Tina, or is it something else?" I asked.

"You better talk to those fucking niggers, Mr. Allen, and tell them to stop calling me a slut!" she demanded.

"Tina, before we go on, I'd recommend you to watch your mouth around me. You know I don't like the swearing or the *N* word," I said.

"Are you going to do something?"

"Did you hear what I said? It was like we were having two totally separate conversations."

"Yeah!"

"Okay. Who are the boys that are calling you names?"

"It's Jerry and his boys," she said with total disdain.

"What are their names?" I wanted to get to the bottom of this one right away.

"I don't know, but you know the other three he hangs out with," she said as she searched for a more visual description.

I was fortunate. It was a Thursday, and on Thursdays I had the use of our student support services coordinator and a couple of probation officers who came into the building to work with some of our kids. I asked Ms. M., our student support services coordinator, to join me on this one. I left Tina with her and I went to get the four boys. The students were all brought together in Ms. M.'s office for a mediation session. Ms. M. began the session by informing the students of the law on sexual harassment.

"Mr. Allen, Mr. Allen!" Jerry shouted.

"Go ahead, Jerry."

Jerry is a unique character. He is nineteen years old and in the ninth grade. He comes to school every day dressed like a homeless man and smelling like weed. His hair is so nappy I'm too scared to be around him when he combs it. I'm scared I might lose an eye due to the flying buckshots. He's the kind of young man who has been in trouble a couple times already this year. The amazing thing about Jerry is that even when he was about to get suspended he always told the truth.

"I'm not sexually harassing anyone," he said in his usual calm, aloof manner.

"Yes you are!" screamed Tina. "You guys have been walking around telling everyone that I will do whatever you ask. Deny that you called me a slut. Deny it."

"Nope," responded Jerry.

"Do the rest of you want to deny that you called Tina a slut?" I asked. The boys just stared at each other and shook their heads.

"Why would you boys want to do something like that?" asked Ms. M. "Can't you see how upset you've made her? This is wrong. This is wrong."

"Well, guys, answer Ms. M., then apologize to Tina," I said.

"Apologize for what?" scorned Jerry.

"Did you hear any of this conversation?" I asked.

"I'm not apologizing to her," Jerry protested.

I responded, "It's either that or be suspended."

"Do you want to know why?" Jerry asked.

"Why?" I asked.

"You don't want me to start talking." Jerry leaned back in his chair as if he had been dealt a royal flush.

"Shut up!" yelled Tina. Ms. M. and I looked at each other knowing the other shoe is about to fall.

Jerry begins pointing at his groin area. "Tell me you weren't sucking on this dick. You followed us home to my boys' crib and we hung out in the basement. You asked me could you suck this dick. Of course I'm gonna say yeah."

"Shut up!"

Jerry continued, "Then after you sucked this dick, you suck his and his and then you dropped your pants and let my boy over there feel you up in front of us."

"You don't have to tell them everything," cried Tina.

"You brought that on yourself."

"You don't have to tell everyone about it," she cried.

"See, Mr. Allen, that's why I'm not apologizing. I was only telling the truth," said Jerry.

"Okay guys, go to my office. Ms. M., I think you need to talk to Tina."

"I think I will," responded Ms. M., who appeared shocked.

As the boys walked out and Ms. M. walked me to the door, I leaned over and whispered, "When did sex become an after school extracurricular activity?"

"Stop it," she said as she shoved me out the door.

I walked the boys back to my office and closed the door behind them as the last one entered.

"Gentlemen, if I asked you to whip it out and rub yourselves on each other, would you?"

"That's sick, Allen," said one of the boys.

"When you get married would you be willing to swap wives every weekend?"

They looked at each other and responded in unison, "No."

"Well guys, it sounds to me like you would. You boys went right down the line, sharing whatever affliction and pathogens each other has. You're nuts and you're lucky."

"Lucky?" one of them asked.

"Tina is a little white girl who sounds sweet and innocent and people who don't know her will listen to her and believe everything she says. Had she screamed rape, your black behinds would be in serious trouble, and the law isn't going to care whether or not your stories match. They would just drop the hammer on four black rapist boys," I warned.

"What's going to happen now?" asked Jerry.

"I'm going to suggest that you guys go to the clinic and get checked out. I can't make you go. Ms. M. and I know the truth now. We will handle the rest of this situation with Tina."

When our students have nothing to do after school, in some cases sex becomes just something to do after school. If schools don't have the recourses to maintain a variety of supervised after-school activities in which students are interested, then students will make up their own extracurricular activities.

CRY FOR HELP

Some childhood dreams should never come true.

I noticed one of my good students writing vigorously in her notebook. That was great, but I was curious to find out why she was doing her work in the middle of the hallway. "Hey kid, what are you working on?" The young lady continued to scribe away. "Do you mind if I take a look?"

The young Haitian girl continues to write. Most people, especially girls, don't want you in their business; but this one was totally ignoring me. I leaned over her and peered at her work. She slowed for a moment, then continued. The first line read: Dear God, why have you forsaken me?

I thought to myself, *Oh boy, you really put your foot into this one. What do I do? What do I do?*

I said to the young lady, "Interesting. Why don't you keep that writing up."

This time she stopped and looked at me then nodded. I figured if she was writing, then she was venting, and I had time to go and get help. A moment later, she continued her task. I walked away slowly and made my left, down the next hall. I then ran my ass off to the student support services coordinator's office.

"Miss M., we have a problem." I said, rushing into her office.

"What is it?"

"We have a young lady who I believe is thinking about hurting herself."

"Are you sure?" She asked.

"Yes. Kids who start off writing about God and 'why have you forsaken me' have got issues." Ms. M. and I walked back to where I left young lady. When we arrived, young lady was still there writing away.

"Hey sweetheart," Ms. M. said to the young lady. Mr. Allen came and got me because he said you were writing some pretty interesting stuff. Do you mind if I take a look?" The young lady stopped and slid her notebook over to Ms. M. "Oh, I see. Why don't you come with Mr. Allen and me to my office so we can talk."

"I don't need to go anywhere!" the young lady screamed.

"We are only here to help you."

"No!"

I'm pretty good at remembering most things but the rest of the incident is a blur. I remember hearing her yell something about her father and being in this country on a dead girl's visa. We had to call a special psychiatric unit. It took four of them and two hours of work to subdue this young lady and bring her to the hospital where she remained for about three weeks.

I've dealt with many suicide situations and letters like this one. Most of those letters went something like the last one I received:

"Those Deemed Worthy"

The names they call me are meant to hurt,
>But they mean nothing anymore.
>My revenge has been planned against those that have taunted,
>Those that believed I was not good enough then.
>The gun is locked and loaded, ready for the assault.
>Ready to cause a silence that no one will ever forget.
>Silence is what I seek

Silence from the deafening remarks that haunt my days.
The names they call me are meant to hurt,
But they mean nothing anymore.
The most popular, the most liked, will be no more.
The hatred that poured out of their every pore
Will be muted when the day is finally through.
They taunted me for the last time this morning.
Those teachers, too, who believe they know who'll succeed, and
who'll fail;
Their trite remarks will cost them their lives.
The names they call me are meant to hurt,
But they mean nothing anymore.
The halls will be full in moments; no one expects a thing.
Those that need to die will gather before me at this given spot;
They always gather here, so here they will die.
The teachers will come too to see what all the noise is about,
And they will join the cold-hearted bitches and bastards.
They'll all gather in hell where they can wonder what they've
done to get there.
The names they called me were meant to hurt,
But they mean nothing anymore.
They're gone now, those taunters and teasers
Never to hurt anyone anymore.
My life's complete, at such a young age,
There is nothing left for me to do,
Except face the music the Creator has in store for me
I won't miss this life when it is done with me.
The names they called me were meant to hurt,
But they mean nothing anymore. . .

The national crime prevention council writes if you observe the following signs then a child may be in danger of hurting themselves or others:

- Lack of interest in school
- Absence of age-appropriate anger control skills

- Seeing self as always the victim
- Persistent disregard for or refusal to follow rules
- Cruelty to pets or other animals
- Artwork or writing that is bleak or violent or depicts isolation or anger
- Talking constantly about weapons or violence
- Obsessions with violent games and TV shows
- Depression or mood swings
- Bringing a weapon (any weapon) to school
- History of bullying
- Misplaced or unwarranted jealousy
- Involvement with or interest in gangs
- Self-isolation from family and friends
- Talking about bringing weapons to school

The young girl who wrote the story said it was just a poem and was no big deal. But what Dylan Klebold and Eric Harris did on April 20, 1999, at Columbine High School in Littleton, Colorado, and what happened to the two school officials and six students at Red Lake High School in Minnesota in 2005, proved that we can't take these situations lightly. It was not a time for me to play deaf nor was it my right to have a judgment call to take her word that it was just a poem and no big deal. A cry for help can turn to screams of horror if left untended. My rule is to never chance it because some childhood dreams should never come true. Learning about depression and suicide is one thing, helping people to be more forthcoming about their condition is another. Depending on the situation, the child should be referred to counseling, peer mediation, gay–straight alliance, or any of the many services available.

SUMMER SCHOOL

Need a butt lift? Start by fixing the ass in the mirror!

"Michael, you know me. I would never come to you unless it is a situation much larger than me."

It was Sarah, a teacher I've grown to love professionally. Because of budget cuts, I lost her at the end of her first year teaching in Boston. She found another job in the system, which was good for somebody, but losing her broke my heart. I was only able to bring her back for this one summer school moment. She is the best English teacher I have ever met. Any teacher who can make really bad kids pick used gum from underneath the desk with their bare hands as a form of punishment for chewing gum in class has my utmost respect. "Sarah, what's going on?"

Sarah began, "It's that student, Neil."

I said, "Tell me what happened."

Sarah doesn't hesitate; but this time she did. "I don't usually get scared, but this time I am. Neil just threatened to kill me."

I got angry. "He did what?"

Sarah continued, "I asked Neil to answer a question about a piece we were reading. He mumbled a curse and slammed his head down on his closed book. I asked him again, calmly but firmly. He stood up and leaned forward, gripping his hands like claws over the front edge of the desk. The effect was menacing."

He then said to me, "You got no idea what I did last night. You mess with me and I will fuckin' kill you."

I began grinding my teeth. "Nobody threatens one of my teachers." I walked out of my office and headed straight into that English class. Neil was sitting right were his teacher left him. I leaned over him and glared. "Come with me."

"Why?" Neil asked.

"Because I said so." Neil reluctantly followed me to the office after he collected his things. During my little walk I managed to calm myself. I chose to whisper my conversation to Neil. "Neil, it is time for us to say good-bye."

"What do you mean?" he asked defiantly.

With that question I knew where this was going and I had to stop it before it went any farther. I had to make a hard decision that I knew was in the best interest of all of the parties. This choice was not easy or ideal. "I mean that your summer school session has come to an end because you are unable to be an appropriate student in school."

"You can't do that," Neil protested.

"I can and I did. Summer school is a privilege, not a right. Your privilege is over, your time here has come to an end."

"I didn't do anything."

"I'm sure if I asked the fourteen witnesses in the class, they would say otherwise. By the way, I'm going to be reporting this incident to your probation officer and I am going to recommend that a new school for you be found. Now good-bye, Neil."

"That ain't right! That's some fuckin' shit!" Neil spat back at the top of his voice.

"Why are you yelling? No one is yelling at you. If you keep it up, I'll have to ask school police to lock you up for disorderly conduct."

Neil stopped and looked around. The one safe place he called his was being taken away. "Mr. Allen, please," he said quietly.

"It's time to say good-bye, Neil. School police and I will walk you out the door."

There would be many meetings to follow about what would be best for Neil. The considerations were an assignment to a different school or a special education placement within and out of the school. Then a decision must be made as to the kind and level of the placement. When considering a special education placement, the questions I always ask myself are, If I send this young black male to special education have I failed him? Have I investigated all avenues before making this referral? Have I ensured that my teachers' expectation of achievement is not insultingly low to the student? There is a disproportionate percentage of African American males in special education and I despise adding more to the list.

Jawanza Kunjufu (1986) expressed it best when he wrote:

> You cannot teach a child who you do not love. You cannot teach a child who you do not respect. You cannot teach a child who you do not understand. You cannot teach a child whom you are afraid of. You cannot teach a child if your "political baggage" i.e. sexism and racism, is brought into the classroom. (How many teachers do you know who have the ability to keep their past experiences about racism and sexism outside the door?) You cannot teach a child without bonding first, which results from love, respect, and understanding. (32)

In the end the right decision was to send Neil to the same school Jay was sent to, where he could get the appropriate services. His requirements were beyond the resources my school could provide.

95

I FORGOT NOT TO GIVE UP

I was made to feel dumb at school until ninth grade. I was in special education (SPED) classes, which meant that I was in the lowest level classes except in math. I remember sitting in earth science class being very bored, when Mr. Flight entered the room. I had Mr. Flight in sixth grade science. He left for the high school after I completed that grade. The man knew his science, and at least he knew how to keep it interesting and alive. Mr. Flight stood by the entrance of the door and watched me doing nothing. After a moment he approached me and began to speak in that deep tone that seemed to vibrate the walls even when he spoke quietly.

"Michael, what are you doing in here?" He asked me.

I looked around the room, picked up my book, and checked the cover and responded, "Taking science."

Mr. Flight grinned and said, "You're getting straight As in here, aren't you?"

"Yes."

"Michael, you know you don't belong in here. You're too smart for this class. If I can arrange it, would you like to take science with

High standards and low expectations
lead to the road of forlorn hope.

me? You won't be getting that easy A anymore, but would you like to earn a solid B?"

"Sure, yeah." I responded eagerly.

Mr. Flight left my table and began talking to my teachers. I could see them looking back and forth at me. There was a nod and Mr. Flight returned. "You'll start on Friday. I'll talk to your mother and guidance counselor today."

Adolescents always harbor a fear that their friends will shut them down and out. But that day in science class my friends said, "You're lucky." By the end of the year, I no longer needed SPED services. I was promoted to a higher level in all of my major subjects, except for math where I was already placed correctly at the higher level. I learned to compensate for my weakness and traded in my image of being that SPED kid to a kid who was going somewhere.

I tell this story because I once forgot what it felt like to be a former SPED student. I had a student in my school that I knew would never pass the Massachusetts Comprehensive Assessment System (MCAS) test. She had taken the test three times and failed. Under normal circumstances, this would seem like no big deal; but she needed to pass this test in order to receive her diploma. She was one of the lowest functioning SPED students I ever encountered. In many ways, she was lucky not to be in a more restrictive environment. I can't tell you that she was a pretty girl. She wore coke bottle glasses and had a nasty scar on the side of her face. But she was one of the nicest girls I had ever met. For months, I told her she could do it. For months, I begged her to concentrate hard. I awarded her the Academy Director's Award for hardest-working student. But in my heart I knew the truth. I spoke to her teachers and they all said, "No way will she pass."

She fooled me. She did pass. I'm embarrassed that I forgot what it was like to be a SPED student. And I'm glad people like Mr. Flight didn't give up on me.

A STORY FROM A FRIEND

Therapy comes in many forms.
Sometimes it comes in conversations with friends.

Michelle is a wonderful person and a great friend. She is a beautiful Latin woman with the brains and fortitude to be successful in whatever she wants to do. We have pushed each other and helped each other see the end of difficult situations. Therapy comes in many forms. Sometimes it comes in formal conversations with friends. Sometimes we just swap the ridiculous.

"Michael," Michelle said on the phone late one evening, "you won't believe what happened today. Are you listening?"

"Yes."

"I had this teacher come into my office today telling me that there is this bad odor coming into his classroom and asked if I would get someone to help. I couldn't believe it was that bad, so I went to check the complaint out. Teachers can exaggerate everything. So, I go to his room and sure enough, it is awful! I swear it's *toxic*. I wanted to tell the class to get out but the smell was so bad I had to run out of the room."

"Did you call someone?" I asked.

"Let me finish. So I'm in the hall. This is seconds later and the bell rings. All of the kids are now in the hallway and that smell is pouring into the school. The hall is crowded, the kids are all screaming 'yuck' and I still can't take the smell. It was bothering me *sooo* bad, I was pushing students out of my way to get to some fresh air. I practically pushed them down the steps as I ran my pregnant ass down two flights of stairs. When I got to the main office, I went right into the principal's office and told him he had to evacuate the building because there are toxic fumes filling the halls. He told me to have a seat and he would check it out."

"You know he called me on the two-way and said he couldn't smell anything. I told him he better sniff again. And then he had the nerve to ask me if this had anything to do with my pregnancy. If it was, then why were all those kids screaming about the smell?"

He just said, "The smell is gone."

"That's it?" I asked.

"No. He then called me a couple of minutes later saying the fumes were back, and he was going to call for help. Then, all of a sudden, the school police called saying they located the source of the smell."

"What was it?" I asked.

"I feel so bad. It was one of the kids in the classroom. He had a stomach virus that must have been festering for weeks. He couldn't control his movement and he went all over himself. I went to go see him, *after* the nurses cleaned him up, and asked him why didn't he come to me for help."

He said, "I tried, but I couldn't catch you. You were moving too fast."

Education, like life, is full of the humorous and the "not so funny." As an administrator, I spend a large portion of my time on the not so funny. The key is not to lose your sense of humor. It is okay to laugh at the humor in the not so funny. Share a funny story with a friend.

ASSISTANT DA BEANED BY BOTTLE

*Dedication through a sea of calm
doesn't require any fortitude.*

Our newly renovated building has become an inviting place. The facade of the building received the same care and attention to detail that went into the innards. The brownstone has been sandblasted to its original 1910 color. The stairs have been resurfaced to a pristine dark cream to match the Romanesque pillars. New brown doors adorn the entrance of the building to finish off the inviting walk past the spring flowers.

"Mr. Allen, Mr. Allen, come here. There's a woman down on the stairs. Someone threw something out the window and it hit her on the head."

I rushed outside and on the granite steps wobbling and slowly getting up was Terry Lang, a twenty-seven-year-old Suffolk County Juvenile Division prosecutor who works out of the Boston office. Apparently someone threw a bottle out of the second floor window; it was still in one piece just a few feet away. I brought Terry inside and called for the nurse and asked someone to get some ice. Terry kept saying she was okay, but it looked to me like she was either experiencing a concussion or at least heading for a healthy headache in the morning.

After the nurse arrived, I ran upstairs to the three classrooms where I suspected the bottle came from. I asked each of the teachers in the room if any students had been near the windows in the past ten minutes. The first teacher said no.

The second teacher in the next classroom said, "What's going on?"

I responded by saying, "I asked you a direct question that requires a yes or a no answer. Then, if it is yes, who was it?"

"No one was by the window," the teacher said.

I walked into the third classroom. It was larger than the others and a substitute teacher was in there for the day. The students, who were mostly minorities, were all sitting quietly in groups of four to six at long brown rectangular tables. I looked at the single window at the opposite end of the room and noticed that it was open, unlike in the other rooms. At that moment, all of the students began to stare at me. I asked the substitute the same question I asked the others and she said she didn't know. I then proceeded to the table nearest the window and asked the boys. "Who threw the bottle?" One student was quick to respond with, "It wasn't me." Then another boy said, "I don't know what you're talking about."

"I'll take that as a sign of guilt," I responded

I then asked the class if they remembered anything. They stated that they noticed a bottle on the windowsill. They then stated that the boys in the back were loud, then all of a sudden became very quiet and the bottle was gone.

The class began to ask what happened.

I responded by saying, "Listen carefully, I don't have a lot of time. Although it looks like I'm trying to get somebody, I'm not. Whoever threw that bottle out of the window hit a white female DA in the head. I repeat, a white DA. In a couple of minutes, the phones will be ringing off the hook, the cops will be here, and they will be looking for somebody's head to roll. I don't think you guys did it on purpose, but if someone doesn't admit to it, the penalty will be much harder if we have to hunt you down."

The class began to point at the last table. A girl in the front of the class then said out loud, "You all better own up to it. Mr. Allen is serious. Mr. Allen, it was someone from that table."

One of my normal troublemakers said, "Damn, Mr. Allen, you see where I'm sittin'. I ain't in it this time."

None of the five boys at the last table said a thing until I said, "Everybody can leave except these five right here."

One boy immediately said, "You can't keep me here. You can't prove I did it."

"I don't need to prove anything. The class said it came from someone at this table and by law that's good enough for me to keep you here. So, at a minimum my friend, that makes you an accomplice. And because no one will own up to it, all of you will go down for it."

"I'm out of here man," said the same boy.

"No you're not. I forgot to tell you that I'm certified to restrain you if I have to; and I've already called school police to join me up here. So even if you did get out of here you wouldn't get far."

On the radio I heard "Mr. Allen, Mr. Allen."

"Go ahead."

"Did you find the kid yet?"

"I have five with me right now. Are you *still* on your way up?"

"Um, I'm on my way up." He caught on and played the game.

I didn't call for school police earlier and this was my only chance to get some backup before they bolted on me.

The students were escorted to the school police office. All five students were asked to give a written statement about the incident. One student wrote:

> I sitting [sic] down in class and "A" said it would be funny to throw a glass out the window. And "A" was scared and I said stop being scared and just throw it. So I tooked [sic] it from him a tossed it out the window. 2 minutes later Allen comes in and asked who threw it. I did not attemp [sic] to throw it at the person. I didn't even look out the window. It was an accident.

Within twenty minutes the head of the DA's office began calling and asking if we caught the student and what was the student's name. He made it quite clear he wanted an arrest. A BPD detective arrested the suspect and that same detective transported him to the area police station.

In a public building filled with over 1,100 hormone-driven students, something is always happening, somewhere. It is impossible to let your guard down, unless you want to get beaned by a bottle.

That year, I completed my five-year project, my educational dream for every high school student. It was to open the first preengineering program in the city. This was my personal high school goal that I achieved. I spent hours planning the room and writing the specifications. In meeting that goal, I felt that I had done everything I could for the main building and I was free to go and start a new chapter in my career. I moved on to take a promotion as academy director/principal. I will now have my own school within a larger school. There will be three others with the same title in the building and one more over us. But what a great opportunity!

THAT TAKES THE CAKE

It was the beginning of February and over my black walkie-talkie
I heard the chatter about an incident in the culinary arts program. Not my area, but I'm bored and I need a little adventure
to brighten my routine day. The quick walk down the beige and orange hall was only impeded by the pushing of the breaker bar on one
of the double doors in the corridors through which I had to pass.

"Mr. Allen, I'm going to need you to write another one of those
no trespassing notices," said my boss. He is a very tall man and well-
known throughout the city. He is actually funny to watch. He is
charismatic and has the bravado to go along with his personality.
CM, as I will call him, is very passionate about our kids. "I know
we're all about the kids, but I'll be . . . if I let that parent in this building again."

"What happened?" I asked.

Mr. S., one of the other academy directors, was standing by. It
was his academy that had the issue with the parent. "I'll tell you. You
won't believe this one. I asked little Shorty to call her mother to pick
her up. That child has been out of control all day and I had enough
of her, you know? So the parent comes upstairs and gets her out of

Some apples just don't fall by a tree. They slam into it.

my office. I thought she took Shorty right out the building, but I guess they smelled the baked goods and couldn't resist. The two of them walked into the bakery and walked behind the counter with the rest of the girls and took the cakes. The chef came out just as they were leaving and yelled out to them and they just started running, with their hands full of cakes."

"You're kidding?" I asked as I shook my head in disbelief.

"No, we're not kidding," said Mr. S. "Hands just full; running out the side door." He reenacted the scene with his hands stretched out as if he were holding the cakes. "I knew I should have escorted them out of the building."

I started to write the letter to the parent explaining that she was no longer welcome in the building, when I found out the security cameras were down in the area. Because of safety concerns, I couldn't ask any of the student witnesses to write a report. Of course when I asked the girl what happened the next day, she claimed the students in the class told her mother that they could take whatever they wanted. With no available witnesses and the security cameras down I couldn't proceed with the notification. (I guess public education is truly free for all.)

How can we teach students about morals when some of their parents don't have any? What is the content of the students' character when their character is under questioning? This is not the kind of knowledge we want to pass down from generation to generation. The Jerry Springerization of American culture is a sure sign that the students of today are kowtowing to the media/hip hop–induced culture promoted by the media. Students often demonstrate a lack of social skills because their parents either lack the skills themselves or have become numb to social norms. This movement has been growing and combining with another dangerous mind-set that promotes letting children freely express themselves. All this creates an extreme society based on self-gratification and entitlement that is devoid of pride. The schools' ethos is and will always be complicated by the ambiguities and contradictions that life's issues manifest in school.

Underlying philosophical and social differences can generate tensions that can be transmitted from one student to many.

Part of an administrator's job is to ensure the consistency of all the rules in the school. Every day, I repeat the same rules and the same expectations to every student, even the rule about not wearing hats. You must lead by example.

"Excuse me young lady, but you need to take that hat off your head."

"It's not that serious, Mr. Allen."

"I didn't ask you that. You just need to take that off your head."

"Damn. Suck my dick."

"You must be gender confused. You don't have one."

"Ha! Mine's bigger than yours."

"Get over here," I told her. The girl ran with her hands flinging through the air. "You can run but you have to come back this way sooner or later!" Damn, she got me good.

"Excuse me, Mr. Allen. Are you busy?" asked a teacher.

"No," I said as I watched my flapping duck run down the hall.

"I can come back if you need to go after her."

"I'm not chasing after her. I'll get her when she comes back through," I said as I continued to look down the hall.

"I just wanted to share something funny with you." The teacher realized I wasn't focused on her and maneuvered to where I had to give her some attention.

Before me is a blond-haired, blue-eyed teacher. She seldom has major issues about anything, so stopping to listen to her is never hard. "Funny is good. What up?"

"I was carrying up some stuff to my classroom and I had a group of boys ask me if I needed any help."

"They said, 'Miss, can we help you? We don't want you to hurt your pretty little hands.'"

"I thanked them for their help and then tried to explain to them why the 'pretty little hands' comment could be considered condescending. Especially considering that this is a vocational school with a lot of girls in it and these girls are very capable of using their hands. They still didn't get it, so I explained it to them again."

"Then one of them said, 'Oh, like you being blond and calling you dumb.'"

"All I could say was, 'Yeah, like that.'"

What takes the cake is having a person responsible for young people's lives lacking a moral compass, for they leave their children directionless. And it happens all the time—from the strangest of places. But from the White House to the outhouse: "Triflin' is trifling."

THE TRICK'S ON YOU

Only conflict and shock can stimulate the realization that your child is correctable.

Kids love Halloween. I hate it. I used to like it as a kid. My brothers and sisters and I would come home with two shopping bags full of candy apiece. We never had to worry about poison in the candy or any other harmful act. In fact, I never saw a trick being performed. I loved getting my own children dressed up and taking them out trick-or-treating. But the trick part has now taken over the fun. One thing is for certain: Halloween tricks and schools don't mix. It takes a strong stance to curb the damage the students gone trickin' can cause.

Every year at Halloween, the school administrators gather at the metal detectors to search the students and their bags. We line the girls on the left and boys on the right. All students must place their bags on the long rectangular table for its special search. The students are asked if there is anything in their bags that doesn't belong there such as eggs and shaving cream. They usually answer with a no, and then we administrators begin. We slap our hands all over the bags, then pick each one up and drop it end over end. (We are prime candidates for working with UPS or as baggage handlers for American Airlines.)

In the fall of 2003, I volunteered to perform a physical search of the boys instead of their book bag. I asked each of them the same question as if I were searching their bags.

"Anything in your pockets such as eggs or cream?"

"Nah," the usual response.

I proceeded to pat their pockets and ask them to open their hands. "Next!"

"Anything in your pockets?"

The student responded, "Yes."

"Like what?"

"I have eggs in my pocket, Mr. Allen," he said nervously.

"Give them up. You know what I'm going to do if you don't," I threatened.

"Am I in trouble?" he asked as he handed me a plastic bag with a half dozen brown eggs in it.

"Yes, you are. Now go over there and wait for me until I get done. Next!"

As the student walked over to where I asked him to stand, Ralph walked up wearing his leather jacket. It was beautifully adorned with patches from many different baseball teams.

"Anything in your pockets?"

"No," said Ralph.

I began the slap and pat. As I moved from the lower part of is jacket to the upper breast pocket, I felt something. "What is this?"

"Nothing," he said as he looked around the foyer.

I grimaced and said, "It feels like something to me. What is it?"

"Nothing."

I squeezed the object a little harder to identify it, and there was a faint pop, followed by a cool, gooey sensation. "I guess you're right. It was nothing," I told him.

"Hey, Mr. Allen!" Mr. Robertson screamed.

"What?" I asked.

"What is he holding behind his back?" asked Mr. Robertson, one of the other administrators. Ralph turned to try and pull himself away. But before he could take a step, the administrative team surrounded him. Ralph hopelessly reached out to hand over his last remaining eggs to the team.

"Ralph, go stand over there by the elevator with that boy." It took another fifteen minutes to get through the rest of the students who were steadily coming in. When I went to pick up the boys with Mr. Robertson, Ralph was missing. "Where is he?" I asked the first boy. The young man shrugged his shoulders. I continued, "Do you want me to let you off easy?"

"Sure," he responded.

"Which way did he go?"

"He went that way," the boy said as he pointed down the stairs that connected to a subterranean gray hallway.

"Mr. Allen," interrupted Mr. Robertson, "what should his consequence be?"

"Give him thirty minutes of detention."

"See how cooperating is so much easier than being negative?" added Mr. Robertson to make the young man feel as if he got off easy.

"Yeah, thanks Mr. A."

I traveled down the hall and caught up with Ralph as he was leaving the locker area. "I told you to wait by the elevator; or did you think you could get away from me?"

"I'd thought I'd give it a try," he said.

I smiled and continued, "Where is your jacket?"

"In my locker," he said, as he pointed in its direction.

"You put a leather jacket with scrambled eggs in the pocket, in a locker, to fester all day. Gross!" I shook my head. I couldn't believe what I was hearing. "Go get it out of there."

Ralph went back to his locker and pulled his jacket out. "Mr. Allen, are you gonna suspend me?"

"Did you run from me?"

He pleaded, "Don't you think the busted eggs in my $400 jacket is enough of a punishment?"

"No. If you hadn't been dishonest with me when I asked you what was in your pocket, it never would have happened."

"I know that now."

I am all for fun! But fun should be had in an arena built for fun, like a rink, a field, or a court. Too often fun, when had in a public setting, spells T-R-O-U-B-L-E B-R-E-W-I-N-G.

WEE ONE

For a change of pace, I decided to work summer school at an elementary school. Even though it is still a job with children, working with little ones and their teachers requires a totally different skill set.

Each morning in this elementary school I greeted every student and I made sure my Student of the Week was still posted in the hallway display. On this particular morning, a small Latina kindergartener was crying. She had light brown hair, lovely brown eyes, and morning breath that would stop a freight train. I stopped performing my daily routine to talk to Wee One.

"Hey sweetheart, what's going on here?" I asked.

"I don't want to be here," she cried.

"Why not? This is such a wonderful place. Don't you like your teachers?"

"Yes. But I just want to go home and go back to bed."

"But you'll miss everything if you do that," I said as I thought about my own desire to go home and go back to bed. Wee One just shrugged her shoulders and continued to cry. I continued, "Listen, why don't you go with your teachers and do me a really big favor?"

From the wee ones to the big ones:
Student–teacher relationships can create a lifetime of beauty.

Wee One sniffled and attempted to stop crying. "When you go to your classroom can you draw me a really pretty picture that I can show off to all of my friends?"

Wee One nodded in agreement.

"Oh that would be so great!" Wee One hurried off to get into line with her classmates, and I felt a little joy knowing that I stopped my first elementary crisis in many years.

At the end of the day, Wee One returned with a smile on her face and a beautiful picture she drew for me. The worst thing I could possibly do would be to not act excited about the personal gift she had drawn for me.

"Ooh, let me see, let me see. This is so beautiful. Thank you." Wee One followed me into the office area and climbed up on a bench as her gleaming brown eyes carefully watched my every move. I took the picture and slid it inside the front cover of my black three-ring binder.

"You like it?" she asked.

"Oh this is wonderful. It feels so good to be loved," I said, rejoicing in a job well done . . . for both of us.

Wee One's eyes twitched as she leaned back as far away from me as she could without falling off the bench. "Hey Mista!"

"What? What's wrong?"

She answered, "I like you, but I don't love you."

Ouch.

An underlying theme in this book, I hope, is about the relationships we build with our students. It is absolutely crucial to the effectiveness of our work. We've got to establish relationships with our students if we expect them to perform, from the wee ones to the big ones. For students watch closely our actions and weigh heavily our words. They make us better administrators and teachers—if we relate with them.

AFTERWORD

I could go on for pages about the ridiculous behaviors I have witnessed and have been forced to participate in and have fixed. Some you may have heard about; and others, maybe not.

Did you hear the one about the girl who posed nude on a porn site? She then shared her pictures with the boys in her class, who then shared them with others throughout the building. She ended up moving out of state.

What about the group of students that beat up and knocked out the front teeth of an innocent boy. He happened to be walking home with another boy he had just met that day, whom the group of students wanted to beat up. The students spent over two years of their lives going in and out of court before three of the five were committed as juvenile offenders.

What about what happened to Neil when he was transferred to a more restrictive school for emotionally disturbed and learning disabled students? The school he moved to happens to have my brother as an administrator. How's that for poetic justice?

I thought these true stories would help you, the reader, understand what it is like to be a teacher or an administrator in an urban environment. These stories are extreme and, for some reason, I've received more than my fair share of them. Even with all of these distractions, it is possible to have great teaching and learning take place. My days are never boring. They are full of stories that read like a song. Each time I go to work, I become a surrogate parent and guardian, even when that is not my intention. I am the judge and jury; I am expected to do no harm, have an unbiased point of view, a low boiling point, and unending compassion which, of course, is rewarded with low pay and honorable status.

An associate justice of the Commonwealth of Massachusetts Appeal Court visited one of the schools I worked in on Law Day and wrote this of the teachers and school:

> Wow—what a challenge. All of the personnel that I met (perhaps ten or a dozen) could not have been more hospitable, professional and plugged in to the task of education. I expect that "education" in many schools of your system must include far more than "reading, writing and 'rithmetic." They may be typical ninth graders everywhere, but I felt some confusion, suspicion, low self-esteem, and all other kinds of social baggage that youngsters carry when they are brought up under disadvantaged circumstances. You and your school people have very important and demanding task. You work much harder than I do!
>
> It was hardly all discouraging, however, I met some bright, enthusiastic and articulate seniors . . . who were introduced to me and told me of the colleges to which they have already been accepted.

In the parlance of the academy, successful teachers and administrators must access their survival kit, which requires the ability to use "near transfer" and "cognitive flexibility" skills. MacPherson defines "near transfer" in his article "Factors Affecting Technological Trouble Shooting Skills" as the ability to apply previously learned knowledge and skills to new situations and contexts that are similar to those in which the learning originally occurred (Johnson and Thomas 1994).

Cognitive flexibility theory was developed by Spiro, Feltovitch, and Coulson (1990). It is largely concerned with the transfer of knowledge and skills beyond the initial learning situation. It is the ability to spontaneously restructure one's knowledge. It is an adaptive response to radically changing situational demands. It's what we administrators do every minute of every day.

It has taken me a lifetime to develop my survival kit. I have learned that teaching and learning is more than theory and philosophy. I have developed distaste for "pound cake" in all its varieties. I had to harness my sixth sense and make it a natural part of my everyday work. I've developed eyes in the back of my head. I'm a great investigator and mediator. My survival kit contains counseling skills such as crisis prevention and violence prevention. I hate admitting it, but at certain times, I must be the dreaded politician, navigating and negotiating between parent and student, student and teacher, and the teacher and the home. I've developed a strange sense of humor that some might even describe as twisted as I search to find the humor in events that aren't so funny. In this kit, I've placed all of my hobbies, accessing them throughout the day as a way to communicate and to build stronger relationships with the kids. With years of experience, I have learned to move and to grow beyond the mistakes I have made. Like a great explorer, I must be prepared for the unexpected storm.

A NOTE FROM A STUDENT

Thanks for always being there, for me to make the right decision. I know that I'm a hard headed, sometimes, but I still listen to what you say. You are the only person that believed in me and kept me on track. You are more than a teacher. You are a friend, a father, and my angel.

Thank you,

Eli

[P.s.] I'm still in school because of your words.

BIBLIOGRAPHY

Albert, Linda.
    1995. *Cooperative Discipline.* Circle Pines, MN: AGS Publishing. www
    .teachersworkshop.com/twshop/cddirty.html.

Attwood, Tony.
    1998. *Asperger's Syndrome.* United Kingdom: Kingsley.

Boston Public Schools.
    2002. *Code of Discipline.* Boston: Boston Public Schools.

Bruner, J. S.
    1956. *A Study of Thinking.* New York: Wiley.

Crisis Prevention Institute.
    2002. *Refresher Workbook: Non Violent Crisis Intervention.* Brookfield,
    WI: Compassion.

Dewey, John.
    1938. *Experience and Education.* Kappa Delta Pi Lecture Series. New
    York: Macmillan.

Festinger, L.
    1957. *A Theory of Cognitive Dissonance.* Stanford, CA: Stanford Uni-
    versity Press. www.gwu.edu/~tip/festinge.html.

Gelzininis, Peter.
1999. "Gang Cop." *Boston Magazine*, May.

Gokhale, Anuradha A.
1995. "Collaborative Learning Enhances Critical Thinking." *Journal of Technology Education*, Fall 1995, 7–1.

Hirsch, E. D., Jr.
1996. "Reality's Revenge: Research and Ideology." *American Educator*, Fall, 6–46.

Johnson, S. D., and Thomas, R. G.
1994. "Implications of Cognitive Science for Instructional Design in Technology Education." *Journal of Technological Studies*, 20, no. 1: 33–44.

Kelley, B. T., Thornberry, T. P., and Smith, C. A.
1997. *In the Wake of Childhood Maltreatment*. Washington, DC: National Institute of Justice.

Kunjufu, Jawan.
1986. *Countering the Conspiracy to Destroy Black Boys*. Vol. 2. Chicago: African American Images.

Lowell Police Department.
2002. *Child Abuse*. www.lowellpolice.com/crime_safety/safety_tips/child_abuse.htm.

MacPherson, R. T.
1998. "Factors Affecting Technological Trouble Shooting Skills." *Journal of Industrial Teacher Education* 35, no. 4.

Meier, D., Chase, B., et al.
2000. *Will Standards Save Public Education?* Boston: Beacon.

National Clearinghouse on Child Abuse and Neglect Information.
2004. *Long-Term Consequences of Child Abuse and Neglect*. http://nccanch.acf.hhs.gov/pubs/factsheets/long_term_consequences.cfm.

National Crime Prevention Council.
2005. *Stopping School Violence*. www.ncpc.org/ncpc/ncpc/?pg=2088-6162.

"The Outspoken Bill Cosby: Comedian Challenges African American Community."
2004. www.cnn.com/2004/SHOWBIZ/TV/11/11/cosby.

Richardson, Franci.
2000. "Teenager Charged in Two-Car Accident, High-Speed Chase." *Boston Herald*, March 27.

Sharma, Mahesh.
1977. *Factors Responsible for Mathematics Learning.* Cambridge: Cambridge University Press.

———.
N.d. *Creativity: Definition, Process, and Methodology to Develop.* Cambridge: Cambridge University Press.

Spiro, R., Feltovitch, P., and Coulson, R.
1990. *Cognitive Flexibility Theory.* www.gwu.edu/~tip/spiro.html.

Sticht, T.
1975–1987. *Functional Context.* www.gwu.edu/~tip/sticht.html.

Widom, C. S., and Maxfield, M. G.
2001. *An Update on the "Cycle of Violence."* Washington, DC: National Institute of Justice.

Zuga, Karen F.
1989. "Relating Technology Education Goals to Curriculum Planning." *Journal of Technology Education* 1. http://borg.lib.vt.edu/ejournals/JTE/jtevlnl/zuga.jte-vlnl.html.

ABOUT THE AUTHOR

Michael Allen was born in Boston, Massachusetts, where he lived with both parents and four siblings. An avid photographer and archer, Allen has been an educator for seventeen years and an administrator for eight. He began his career as a paraprofessional and worked his way up through the ranks. He's currently employed as an academy director/principal in a vocational school specializing in the technology fields. Michael also taught as a special topics faculty instructor at University of Massachusetts–Boston. His passion has always been to bring engineering and other high-tech areas into public education to help students improve their cognitive skills, stemming from his work as an industrial arts teacher instructing in woodworking, graphics, and computer-aided design. Michael has a master of education degree from Cambridge College and a certificate of advanced graduate study from Bridgewater State College.

Made in the USA
Middletown, DE
02 February 2020